# British Contested History

Caroline Donnellan

# British Contested History

## Place and Space

Place and Space

Caroline Donnellan
Boston University Global Programmes
London, UK

ISBN 978-3-031-62208-3        ISBN 978-3-031-62209-0   (eBook)
https://doi.org/10.1007/978-3-031-62209-0

This Palgrave Macmillan imprint is published by the registered company Springer Nature Switzerland AG.
The registered company address is: Gewerbestrasse 11, 6330 Cham, Switzerland

Paper in this product is recyclable.

# CONTENTS

1  Introduction: British Contested History—Place and Space      1
   *Introduction: British Contested History*                     2
   *Geography and History: Space and Place*                      3
   *Contested History or Critical Heritage?*                     4
   *Britain's Overseas' Heritage*                                5
   *Chapter Synopsis*                                            7
   *References*                                                  9

2  The Spaces of Writing the Past: Historicising the Nation     13
   *Introduction: History and the Past*                         14
   *Historiography*                                             15
   *English and British History*                                17
   *Historicising the Nation*                                   20
   *Nostalgising the Past and the Post-War Country House Novel*  22
   *References*                                                 25

3  Whitehall: Places of History and State Spaces               31
   *Introduction: The Palace of Whitehall*                      32
   *The Spaces of the Divine Right of Kings*                    33
   *Building the Empire—Building Whitehall*                     37
   *A Place of Remembrance*                                     39
   *State Spaces: Whitehall 2020—Black Lives Matter*            40
   *References*                                                 42

**4    Greece and Mesopotamia in Britain: Changing Places    47**
*Introduction: Contested History and Critical Heritage*    48
*A Sense of Place: Athens*    49
*The Parthenon Sculptures in Britain*    51
*Changing Places: Mesopotamia and Britain*    53
*Reconstructing Mesopotamia in the Early Twentieth Century*    55
*Archaeology and a Conflicted Present*    57
*References*    60

**5    Liverpool: The Spaces of Remembering and the Places of Forgetting Again    65**
*Introduction: Haunted Histories*    66
*Maritime Liverpool*    67
*The Infrastructure of Place*    69
*The Twentieth Century*    70
*Reinventing Liverpool: New Placemaking*    73
*References*    76

**Index**    81

# Introduction: British Contested History— Place and Space

**Abstract** This chapter introduces the issues relating to British contested history by considering how it came to be constructed, how it developed, and how, over time, attitudes are beginning to change towards it. The history began when the nation's grand narrative was being written. What it created is a difficult trajectory for a modern nation. Adding to this complex situation is the relationship between British history and the past. Why this is problematic is because the words history and the past are sometimes used interchangeably to mean the same thing, when they are not. To unpack these different positions this interdisciplinary research is underpinned by spatial relations. Why? Following the third post-pandemic spatial turn, place was repositioned alongside space which brought new insights into the academic field concerning questions of location and mapping. This research, therefore, considers the sometimes antagonistic relationship between the places of history and the spaces of the past. The corresponding research questions are: what role does place and space play in historical constructions of the past? How do place and space contribute to contested history? Can contested historic places and spaces be remapped and endowed with new meanings? Conclusively, it asks is there another way to address the fact that Britain is no longer rooted to the idea of one history and one past?

**Keywords** Britain • Contested History • Critical Heritage • Geography • Place • Space • The Spatial Turn

C. Donnellan, *British Contested History*, https://doi.org/10.1007/978-3-031-62209-0_1

1

## INTRODUCTION: BRITISH CONTESTED HISTORY

History is the curation of the past. In this act of selecting, editing, and organising, it turns the past into a story 'which is thought to possess a discernible beginning, middle, and end' (White, 1973, p. 5). In this production of the past, certain events are expunged which results in one voice that neither responds to how life was nor is. Within this cause-and-effect model of 'historical inevitability' the way life happens could not happen any other way (Nagel, 1960, p. 291). How history does this is by carving the past into 'temporal structures and concepts' which are turned into periods, eras, and epochs (Hölscher, 2014, p. 577). Unlike the determinism of history, the past is stochastic with its unpredictability; it is about things happening more by chance than design. History's response is that it is analytical and rigorously archived, yet the writers of history rarely acknowledge the role that subjectivity plays in determining their outcomes. History can, however, enlighten previously vanquished areas that may better inform the present, and is why Sally Alexander and Barbara Taylor assert: 'Historians explore the many ways that the past survives within the present—as institutions, myths, habits of thought, or silences; they show how that which has been forgotten may yet influence some of the most recalcitrant problems of an age' (Alexander & Taylor, 2012, p. 2).

When considering the ideological position of British history, 'wide-ranging accounts of the limits as well as the possibilities of empire's method on the ground' must be addressed (Burton, 2015, p. 8). These imperial narratives remain overtly or more obliquely embedded within history. One of history's sites is the historic environment which continues to communicate its ideological basis through 'urban memory and performance' (Hopkins & Orr, 2009, p. 47). The more visible demonstrations are witnessed in official state places and in a less explicit way in the wider built historic environment. For this reason, independent agencies and research institutes are re-assessing these sites. These include the Contested Histories Initiative (CHI) which investigates how 'Statues, monuments, street names, and other markers project a collective historical memory on public space' (Contested Histories, 2024, https://contestedhistories.org/). While the CHI identifies there is more than one history, *British Contested History: Place and Space* addresses them in the singular on the basis they are complicit within the same narrative. The aim is to unpack why and where this history began through an interdisciplinary approach that draws on architecture, heritage, history, historiography, literature, philosophy, and urban studies. The methodology is through human geography which Tim Creswell describes in its fundamental form as 'the study of places' (Creswell, 2004, p. 1). Why this is important is because '*where* things happen is critical to knowing *how* and *why* they happen' (Warf & Arias, 2009, p. 1).

## GEOGRAPHY AND HISTORY: SPACE AND PLACE

The turning point in the social sciences and the humanities was the publication of Yi-Fu Tuan's *Space and Place: The Perspective of Experience* (1977). In exploring how space and place are experienced and affected by time, this opened up the field of human geography. Earlier, Henri Lefebvre's *The Production of Space* (1974) conflated space and place as 'social space' (Lefebvre, 1991, p. 1). Tuan reset space and place as related but different fields. The spatial turn that followed in the 1980s saw other academic disciplines, including historical studies, drawing on place as a methodological approach. John Barrell's *The Dark Side of the Landscape: The Rural Poor in English Painting 1730–1840* (1980) argues that the urban poor were exploited by the landscape in which they lived and worked. Representing social realism was never the intention of the landscape artists who painted it. They included John Constable, the son of a well-off East Anglian mill owner. The idea of representing the reality of things 'would have been a considerable embarrassment to Constable, in his attempt to recreate an older georgic, image of the fat and productive land of East Anglia' (Barrell, 1980, p. 134). While Barrell's work reverberated with the first spatial turn, the idea of place remained relegated to a subordinate role.

The reticence towards acknowledging the centrality of place is examined in Edward S. Casey's *The Fate of Place: A Philosophical History* (1997), in which he states 'place is so much with us, and we with it, it has been taken for granted, deemed not worthy of separate treatment' (Casey, 1997, p. x.). Casey's aim is to reveal 'the concealed history of place' (Casey, 1997, p. x.). This proved more difficult than imagined because regarding the wider spatial turn—place remained as it were—in the same place. A second post-millennium spatial turn was declared in Barney Warf and Santa Arias's *The Spatial Turn: Interdisciplinary Perspectives* (2009). 'Recent works in the fields of literary and cultural studies, sociology, political science, anthropology, history, and art history have become increasingly spatial in their orientation' (Warf & Arias, 2009, p. 1). Despite this

assertion, place continued to be assigned to a secondary position in relation to space. Why? 'Since Plato, Western philosophy […] has enshrined
space as the absolute, unlimited and universal while banning place to the
realm of the particular, the limited, the local, and the bound' (Escobar,
2001, p. 143). When place came to the fore was during the COVID–19
pandemic lockdowns of 2020–2021. The impact saw different environ-
ments connecting through a range of videotelephony software including
Zoom, and Voov with other places, and as they did—a third, virtual, spatial turn revealed itself.

Why the third virtual, spatial turn is important is because it demonstrated place and connecting to place matters. We are born in place, we
live in place, we work in place, and we die in place. What is fundamental
to understanding place is that it changes and nowhere is this better under-
stood than in returning to a childhood home as an adult. Place is, therefore, rooted in the 'locale, "the local," or localness'—and while it is about
more than this—its cornerstone is location (Withers, 2009, p. 638). It is
for this reason that place is determined through 'the experience of a particular location' (Escobar, 2001, p. 140). Alternatively, as Creswell points
out, 'Space is a more abstract concept than place' (Creswell, 2004, p. 8).
Space is where we think, where we imagine, where we remember, and
where we forget again. Space does not have the assurance of place and is
why Tuan claims: 'Place is security, space is freedom: we are attached to
the one and long for the other' (Tuan, 1977, p. 3). With these polarities
in mind, this book explores the intersection between the conceptual spaces
of the past and the physical places of history to consider how they fit with
a modern vision of Britain.

## Contested History or Critical Heritage?

A further point relating to the places of history and the spaces of the past
is the overlap between contested history and critical heritage. The UCL
Centre for Critical Heritage Studies states its aim is to interpret 'evolving,
multi-scalar forms of heritage and identity issues of heritage justice' (UCL
Centre for Critical Heritage Studies, 2024, https://www.ucl.ac.uk/
critical-heritage-studies/centre-critical-heritage-studies). Critical heritage, therefore, engages with changing narratives. Dallen J. Timothy and
Stephen W. Boyd provide a useful outline of heritage's existing narratives.
'Heritage can be classified as tangible immoveable resources (e.g. buildings, rivers, natural areas); tangible moveable resources (e.g. objects in

museums, documents in archives); or intangibles such as values, customs, ceremonies, lifestyles, and including experiences such as festivals, arts and cultural events' (Timothy & Boyd, 2003, p. 3). The conundrum is that these heritage resources are historical in their construction, and it is for this reason that there is an overlap between the two areas. An example of this is Neil Brodie, Jenny Doole, and Peter Watson's *Stealing History: The Illicit Trade in Cultural Material* (2002) which investigates how the illegally excavated Iron Age Salisbury Hoard in Wiltshire in 1985 was dispersed. 'Many dealers and auction houses—including Sotheby's, Christie's and Spinks—at one time or other sold objects from this hoard, not knowing them to be stolen of course' (Brodie et al., 2002, p. 29). While their research focuses on the illicit removal and subsequent trade in material heritage, the thesis is on stealing history.

The question is should a line be drawn between contested history and critical heritage, and why has it become an issue? John Carman argues: 'Much of this literature is concerned with defining "heritage" as something separate from "history" or the "real" past' (Carman, 2002, p. 2). The aim of history, as will be discussed, began as an inquiry, a record of the past, and then turned into a study of the past. The aim of heritage is more complex, in that there is less consensus about what it is and is why Carman adds: 'The heritage field is something about which little simple agreement exists. [...] It is made up of physical material that can just as easily be classed as something other than heritage—as history, as archaeology, as architecture, as art or, indeed, as nature' (Carman, 2002, p. 22). A further issue relating to heritage is that it 'creates identity' (Albert et al., 2022, p. 4). Why this is problematic is because while Britain may wish to have one identity and one voice, it has many, and it is for this reason why British history and the heritage relating to it have become a contested one.

## Britain's Overseas' Heritage

A further issue relating to British history and heritage is its complex relationship with other nation's history and heritage. For example, the Benin Bronzes were 'taken under the conditions of duress that were ever-present under colonialism' (Hicks, 2020, p. 19). In 1897 they were removed from the royal palace of the Kingdom of Benin, which is today southern Nigeria. The British colonial appropriation that Dan Hicks identifies leads to the further issue of site displacement, which is important because debates on overseas heritage tend to be eclipsed by the question of ownership. The

Benin Bronzes and many other artefacts listed on the British Museum's Accessions Register were displaced from their sites of origin and are now in London. What is noteworthy is how a relatively small island, Britain, off the north-west coast of Europe felt entitled to appropriate other nations' possessions. Dimitris Tziovas asserts: 'A nation or a country can be judged by the way it engages with its past and its memories' (Tziovas, 2014, p. 1). A nation can also be judged by the way it engages with other nations' pasts and memories. Due to the mounting debates concerning contested history and international critical heritage, Britain is attracting polarised points of view, and because of this, there is the need for more focused scholarly research in the field.

The available literature includes Bernard Porter's *Britain's Contested History: Lessons for Patriots* (2022), which addresses the themes of imperialism and Brexit from a postcolonial and pro-European Union perspective. Porter is keen to emphasise that this is neither a 'celebratory' nor 'hyper-critical' account of the nation, but it does critique aspects of Britain's contested history (Porter, 2022, p. vi). A further publication echoing a postcolonial perspective is John Thieme's *Postcolonial Literary Geographies: Out of Place* (2016). The core proposition is that in the 'era of exploration, trade, conquest and missionary activity, imperialist practices and more recently neo-colonial forms of globalization have habitually promoted fixed conceptions of place, while redrawing borders, dispossessing peoples and despoiling landscapes for commercial gain' (Thieme, 2016, p. 2). The problem he identifies is that in creating one dominant narrative revolving around the nation's place in history has led to issues concerning the place of the environment, disadvantaged peoples, animal rights, and ecology.

An earlier publication focusing on place in relation to history is David N. Livingstone's *The Geographical Tradition: Episodes in the History of a Contested Enterprise* (1992). In providing a 'history of the geographical tradition,' this is relevant to this research because it signposts how geography played a defining role in the narrative of contested history (Livingstone, 1992, p. 31). Geography's agents include mainly European cartographers, explorers, navigators, biologists, naturalists, and scientists who have mapped, and categorised, the known world. What they documented was always beneficial to their own nations rather than those they colonised, conquered, and Christianised. A later publication that addresses the complexity that has emerged because of this historical situation is Daniel J. Walkowitz and Lisa Maya Knauer's edited *Contested Histories in Public*

*Space: Memory, Race, and Nation* (2009). The authors explore how contemporary global issues have been created by 'the existence of fundamental conflicts over the interpretation of history and its representation in the public arena' (Knauer & Walkowitz, 2009, p. 3). This book shares the preceding ideas and, along with a re-appraisal on the re-interpretation of history, it is also about re-aligning the critical role of the past. Where it bridges a gap is that it addresses the places of history in relation to the spaces of the past.

## CHAPTER SYNOPSIS

The aim of this chapter, 'Introduction. British Contested History: Place and Space,' is to address how these areas can bring clear insights into a complex field of research. Drawing on the work of Ethan Kleinberg, the objective is 'to advocate for a revaluation of these boundaries and our strategies for thinking and writing about the past' (Kleinberg, 2017, p. 1). On this basis, this is more than a book about contested history, it is about repositioning the fundamental role of the past. It does this through the places of history and the spaces of the past which includes writing. Chapter 2, 'The Spaces of the Writing the Past: Historicising the Nation,' therefore, examines how the early construction of history began with the writing of Herodotus. The Greek historian was soon castigated, however, for including 'story elements that do not seem to us, strictly speaking, historical, but rather to have sprung from the world of earlier Greek thinking' (Dewald, 2012, p. 60). The model provided by Thucydides with its facts and analysis became the template for modern history which synthesised with the later Anglo-Saxon histories, and those that followed saw an official account of British history emerge. By the mid-twentieth century, this model was challenged. With the onslaught of the New Left and Modernism, there was a post-war move to preserve the past. Where this was enacted was through the historic environment, and in literature through the country house novel which was about 'eulogizing a time' in Britain's past (Henderson, 2017, p. 715). This chapter examines why these shifting positions to British history and the past are being re-assessed in a new light.

Chapter 3, 'Whitehall: Places of History and State Spaces,' examines how a royal palace was established for the Tudor court. At the beginning of the seventeenth century, Whitehall Palace became the London residence for the new Stuart dynasty. Towards the end of the century a constitutional monarchy was declared which through the Bill of Rights (1689) 'sought, not to limit the powers of government or parliament, but to limit the powers of the sovereign' (Bogdanor, 1995, p. 5). The eighteenth century saw the establishment of the United Kingdom of Britain and an expanding state at Whitehall which functioned as the hub of a 'capital city of a world-wide empire' (Port, 1995, p. 1). Post-Empire when Black Lives Matter protestors marched through Whitehall the question the action raised is: does the historic context need to be reset to better fit with a modern vision of Britain? Chapter 4, 'Greece and Mesopotamia in Britain: Changing Places,' discusses the appropriation of overseas nations' heritage which includes the Parthenon sculptures and Mesopotamian antiquities. When these antiquities arrived in the British Museum, they 'presented an unsettling addition to a history of ancient art and cultures whose primary touchstones had been objects from ancient Egypt and the Greco-Roman world' (Bohrer, 1998, p. 336). As a hierarchy of old-world cultures emerged, so did questions of site displacement and ownership. The outcome today is that while the British Museum is under pressure to return various antiquities, its position remains that it is a universal museum which acts as the keeper of world cultures. Yet these collections are not in the world they are in London because what 'matters is location' (Evans, 2001, p. 218). The question is how can this contested history and overseas material heritage be resolved?

Chapter 5, 'Liverpool: The Spaces of Remembering and the Places of Forgetting Again,' identifies how the Industrial Revolution is woven into the fabric of the nation to the extent its heritage has become 'an integral part of our culture' (Loures, 2008, p. 688). What else is integral is the relationship between the Industrial Revolution, the Empire, and the slave trade. This chapter looks at how the Port of Liverpool benefitted from transatlantic trading. Liverpool's maritime activities which included the slave trade went in tandem with the city's expansion through its public buildings and private houses in the Merchant's quarter. Modern Liverpool has been able to capitalise on its past and, after London, hosts the second-largest number of art galleries, national museums, listed buildings, and listed parks in Britain. Liverpool City Council aims, however, to attract visitors to a more sanitised account of its past. 'Abstracted and redeployed, history seems to be purged of political tension; it becomes a unifying spectacle, the settling of all disputes. [...] the national past occurs in a dimension of its own—a dimension in which we appear to remember only in order to forget' (Wright, 2009, p. 65). Considering Patrick Wright's assertion concerning Liverpool and all sites of contested history, this chapter, and the rest of the book, addresses why it is important to remember the spaces of the past, and not to forget them again through the places of history.

## REFERENCES

Albert, M.-T., Bernecker, R., Cave, C., Prodan, A. C., & Ripp, M. (2022). Introduction into the Overall Message of the Book: Destruction of Heritage Is Destroying Identity—Shared Responsibility Is Therefore Our Common Task for the Future. In M.-T. Albert, R. Bernecker, C. Cave, A. C. Prodan, & M. Ripp (Eds.), *50 Years World Heritage Convention: Shared Responsibility—Conflict & Reconciliation* (pp. 3–20). Springer. https://doi.org/10.1007/978-3-031-05660-4

Alexander, S., & Taylor, B. (2012). Introduction. In S. Alexander & B. Taylor (Eds.), *History and Psyche: Culture, Psychoanalysis, and the Past* (pp. 1–10). Palgrave Macmillan. https://doi.org/10.1057/9781137092427

Barrell, J. (1980). *The Dark Side of the Landscape: The Rural Poor in English Painting 1730–1840*. Cambridge University Press.

Bogdanor, V. (1995). *The Monarchy and the Constitution*. Clarendon Press/Oxford University Press. https://doi.org/10.1093/0198293348.001.0001

Bohrer, F. N. (1998). Inventing Assyria: Exoticism and Reception in Nineteenth Century England and France. *The Art Bulletin, 80*(2), 336–356. https://doi.org/10.2307/3051236

Brodie, N., Doole, J., & Watson, P. (2002). *Stealing History: The Illicit Trade in Cultural Material*. The McDonald Institute for Archaeological Research.

Burton, A. (2015). *The Trouble with Empire: Challenges to Modern British Imperialism*. Oxford University Press.

Carman, J. (2002). *Archaeology and Heritage: An Introduction*. Continuum.

Casey, E. S. (1997). *The Fate of Place: A Philosophical History*. University of California Press.

Contested Histories. (2024). (To Unite or to Divide?) https://contestedhistories.org/

Creswell, T. (2004). *Place: A Short Introduction* (1st ed.). Blackwell Publishing.

Dewald, C. (2012). Myth and Legend in Herodotus' First Book. In E. Baragwanath & M. de Bakker (Eds.), *Myth, Truth, and Narrative in Herodotus* (pp. 59–86). Oxford University Press. https://doi.org/10.1093/acprof:oso/9780199693979.003.0002

Escobar, A. (2001). Culture Sits in Places: Reflections on Globalism and Subaltern Strategies of Localization. *Political Geography, 20*(2), 139–174. https://doi.org/10.1016/s0962-6298(00)00064-0

Evans, J. A. (2001). The Parthenon Marbles—Past and Future. *Contemporary Review, 279*(1629), 212–218.

Henderson, K. C. (2017). New Britain, Old England: Heritage Renewed in Atonement. *Modern Fiction Studies, 63*(4), 714–736. https://doi.org/10.1353/mfs.2017.0054

Hicks, D. (2020). *The Brutish Museums: The Benin Bronzes, Colonial Violence and Cultural Restitution.* Pluto Press. https://doi.org/10.4000/ceroart.8297

Hölscher, L. (2014). Time Gardens: Historical Concepts in Modern Historiography. *History and Theory, 53*(4), 577–591. https://doi.org/10.1111/hith.10732

Hopkins, D. J., & Orr, S. (2009). Memory/Memorial/Performance: Lower Manhattan, 1776/2001. In D. J. Hopkins, S. Orr, & K. Solga (Eds.), *Performance and the City* (pp. 33–50). Palgrave Macmillan. https://doi.org/10.1007/978-0-230-30521-2

Kleinberg, E. (2017). *Haunting History: For a Deconstructive Approach to the Past.* Stanford University Press. https://doi.org/10.1515/9781503603424

Knauer, L. M., & Walkowitz, D. J. (2009). Introduction: Memory, Race, and the Nation in Public Spaces. In D. J. Walkowitz & L. M. Knauer (Eds.), *Contested Histories in Public Space: Memory, Race, and Nation* (pp. 1–27). Duke University Press. https://doi.org/10.1215/9780822391425

Lefebvre, H. (1991). *The Production of Space* (D. Nicholson-Smith, Trans.). Blackwell Publishing.

Livingstone, D. N. (1992). *The Geographical Tradition.* Blackwell Publishing.

Loures, L. (2008). Industrial Heritage: The Past in the Future of the City. *WSEAS Transactions on Environment and Development, 4*(8), 687–696.

Nagel, E. (1960). Determinism in History. *Philosophy and Phenomenological Research, 20*(3), 291–317. https://doi.org/10.2307/2105051

Port, M. H. (1995). *Imperial London: Civil Government Buildings in London 1851–1915.* Yale University Press.

Porter, B. (2022). *Britain's Contested History: Lessons for Patriots.* Bloomsbury Academic. https://doi.org/10.5040/9781350296411

Thieme, J. (2016). *Postcolonial Literary Geographies: Out of Place.* Palgrave Macmillan. https://doi.org/10.1057/978-1-137-45687-8

Timothy, D. J., & Boyd, S. W. (2003). *Heritage Tourism.* Prentice Hall.

Tuan, Y. (1977). *Space and Place: The Perspective of Experience.* University of Minnesota Press.

Tziovas, D. (2014). Introduction: Decolonizing Antiquity, Heritage Politics, and Performing the Past. In D. Tziovas (Ed.), *Re-imagining the Past: Antiquity and Modern Greek Culture* (pp. 1–26). Oxford University Press. https://doi.org/10.1093/acprof:oso/9780199672752.003.0001

UCL Centre for Critical Heritage Studies. (2024). (Centre for Critical Heritage Studies). https://www.ucl.ac.uk/critical-heritage-studies/centre-critical-heritage-studies

Warf, B., & Arias, S. (2009). Introduction: The Reinsertion of Space in the Humanities and the Social Sciences. In B. Warf & S. Arias (Eds.), *The Spatial Turn: Interdisciplinary Perspectives* (pp. 1–10). Routledge. https://doi.org/10.4324/9780203891308

White, H. (1973). *Metahistory: The Historical Imagination in Nineteenth–Century Europe*. The John Hopkins University Press.

Withers, C. W. J. (2009). Place and the "Spatial Turn" in Geography and in History. *Journal of the History of Ideas, 4*(4), 637–658. https://doi.org/10.1353/jhi.0.0054

Wright, P. (2009). *On Living in an Old Country: The National Past in Contemporary Britain*. Oxford University Press.

## CHAPTER 2

# The Spaces of Writing the Past: Historicising the Nation

**Abstract** Writing the past begins with history. Writing British history began before Britain was Britain. When Herodotus provided the first formal inquiry into the past, he was castigated for drawing on myth and imagination. The model provided by Thucydides focused instead on factual events and their analysis. The later Anglo-Saxon histories contributed to a different kind of retelling of the past that sometimes veered to the miraculous and the legendary. With the histories that followed fused with the Thucydidean model what emerged was the official account of the British nation. The turning point was during the post-war period when Clement Attlee's Labour government created a more socialist vision of Britain. One of the areas this was reflected in was in the writing of history, and as the revised Marxist approach rejected the existing top-down model it asserted itself as the new reliable narrator. What it re-established, however, was the same template, albeit from a different perspective which is when we do history, we already know the end. This chapter begins therefore by looking at the history of history, concerning how it developed and impacted on writing the British narrative. It explores how when there was a shift to Modernism there was a counter-offensive to preserve the past. Where this was demonstrated was in the historic environment and in the post-war country house novel. What these changing attitudes reflect is that the past is not a settled agenda. The question is, if we are to continue with this model of history, how might we begin to do it better?

**Keywords**  History • Historiography • Myth • Writing • Narrative • Preservation

## INTRODUCTION: HISTORY AND THE PAST

The original aim of history was to provide an inquiry into the past, this changed when it turned into something more ubiquitous in becoming that thing that would explain everything. How this was achieved was by creating the idea that there is a linear progression from the past to the present, as if working to a kind of cosmic time clock. An alternative way of thinking about the past and the present is proposed by Simone de Beauvoir. 'The present is a transitory existence which is made in order to be abolished' (de Beauvoir, 2018, p. 126). While the abolished part of the present is the past, the question is where is history in this relationship? Walter Benjamin reminds us: 'History is the study of a structure whose site is not homogenous, empty time, but time filled by the presence of the now [*Jetztzeit*]' (Benjamin, 2015, pp. 252–253). In being filled by the presence of now, history is about two things: (1) the period that the history is being written in; (2) the period that the history is being written about. In its written construction, history is about the relationship with its reader who is 'the space on which all the quotations that make up a writing are inscribed' (Barthes, 1977, p. 148). What results are many readers and many pasts. The problem is that while history provides different interpretations of the past, it remains tied to the idea of there being one past.

This chapter looks at how the historical paradigm was created and considers why the first method of inquiry was rejected on the basis that 'history was not intended to make pleasurable reading, but it was to tell the truth' (Evans, 1968, p. 11). It explores the issues that have emerged from the cause-and-effect model which supports a top-down homogenous trajectory, as Priya Satia asserts: 'For much of the modern period, historians have not been critics but abettors of those in power' (Satia, 2020, p. 1). When the model was re-evaluated, the revisionists replaced it with their own one, and in doing so, repositioned themselves in the role of the reckoner in relation to the thing to be reckoned with. As the old model was challenged another agent of history, the historic environment responded through preservation groups campaigning against its modernising forces. A further counter-offensive was through the nostalgising themes of the post-war country house novel. Due to these changing positions, the question is: is there another way to engage with the past? On this point Lucien Hölscher asserts: 'The past is no longer seen as something stable, but rather as a changing projection of the present and future' (Hölscher, 2013, p. 139). Is it time, therefore, to accept that the past is not detached from the present and that a new kind of historiography is required, and while this is not about the end of history it is about broadening its horizons.

## HISTORIOGRAPHY

The history of history begins with historiography. While historiography is the writing of history, it has also come to mean the study of the writing of history. The word history derives from the ancient Greek *historía* meaning inquiry. The first formal historical inquiry was proposed by the Greek historian Herodotus whose work *The Histories* (c. 430 BC) recounts the Greco-Persian wars. His method was through the investigation of sources with the intention that history has 'to record' (Herodotus, 2003, p. 145). Herodotus was also a geographer and would have been keenly aware of the idea of place, coming from the Greek city of Halicarnassus, which is present-day Bodrum in Turkey. While Herodotus later garnered a reputation as *the father of history*, the validity of his work was questioned due to the kinds of events and spaces he addressed in his writing. Foremost, Herodotus was accused of being fanciful, an example of this includes how 'a dolphin picked up Arion and carried him on its back to Taenarum' (Herodotus, 2003, p. 11). The question is: did Herodotus believe this or was he more interested in it as a trope, and the idea of myth with its limitless ways of thinking about the world? A different approach was taken by the Athenian Thucydides who 'did not allow his mind to wander into barren speculations, but kept it with unswerving, steadfastness' (Cochrane, 1929, p. 15).

Thucydides's *History of the Peloponnesian War* (431 BC–404 BC) states that he drew on eyewitness accounts, facts, and analysis, yet similarly to Herodotus uses his imagination. Thucydides's work was also challenged, which is addressed by Zachary Sayre Schiffman. 'Arguably the greatest of all historians, Thucydides remains at best intensely difficult for modern readers and at worst utterly boring' (Schiffman, 2011, p. 16). The question is: was Thucydides a reliable author? The question of authenticity did not plague his work in the way it persisted with Herodotus, which continued into the late twentieth century, as evidenced in Donald Lateiner's critique: 'Herodotus prizes artful deception and quick-thinking acts that promote self-preservation' (Lateiner, 1990, p. 231). Is Herodotus's work deceptive on the basis he is not telling the truth and if so, who is telling the truth? Invariably, it is the historian who always shapes the truth no matter how factual and keenly observed their scholarly musings may appear. Is it the right, therefore, for the historian to admonish Herodotus when their work proceeds from their version of the truth? In the twenty-first century, Herodotus's critics continued to wade into the argument that his work is delusory in extending 'to much that is marvellous for its own sake, not for what it explains' (Pelling, 2019, p. 2). Is history meant to explain or was Herodotus providing his own way of making sense of what was around him?

> Herodotus's own world, that of a Greek-speaking elite, was a highly literate one, though still mainly reliant on oral tradition for its knowledge of the past. [...] But it was clearly a world buzzing with rival oral traditions and orally transmitted, formulaic popular tales; with legends and accounts of mythic beasts, peoples, and countries; with stories of foundlings, tests, tricks, subterfuges, riddles, and prophetic dreams. (Burrow, 2008, p. 16)

Where John Burrow situates Herodotus's writing is in the vernacular by arguing that he drew on the motif of myth as a parallel literary device which his contemporary readers would have been familiar with. In the same way, today, we use a metaphor as an idiom to elaborate on the meaning of a thing. Within this convention, a metaphor is used in the knowledge that it is a metaphor. For example, the British expression *it is raining cats and dogs* means it is raining heavily, there is nothing mystical nor 'supernatural' about it, yet this argument continues to interrogate Herodotus's writings (Cochrane, 1929, p. 107). Furthermore, everyday language today is far removed from the august tones of academic historical writing. When Herodotus was writing, there were no formal conventions for academic historical writing but there were the conventions of everyday speech. Yet Herodotus's approach remains unacceptable within the conventions prescribed by modern historians in their fervour 'to conduct research, engage in intellectual debate, and advance interpretations of the past' (Landsberg, 2015, p. 1).

## ENGLISH AND BRITISH HISTORY

The later English and British histories went through their own permutations of writing the past. These include Bede's *Ecclesiastical History of the English People* (c. 731 AD) in which he provides a chronicle of Christianity in England from the Roman period to his own time. What he produced was for 'a predominantly elite monastic group' (Gunn, 2009, p. 36). Elite or otherwise, in writing for a religious audience, the chronicle includes elements of the miraculous and is why Marnie Hughes-Warrington asserts: 'Bede narrated a history of the English church and the Anglo Saxon people in which remarkable events abound' (Hughes-Warrington, 2019, p. 28). A further consideration is that while Bede's account also serves as a social history, much of the writing is about an earlier period when his own resources concerning that time would have been limited. A different account of England and Britain's past is provided in Geoffrey of Monmouth's *Historia Regum Britanniae—The History of the Kings of Britain*, (c. 1136), which chronicles two thousand years of history. Julia Crick assesses his work in relationship to history. 'Among Geoffrey's greater departures from historical credibility is his championship of two mythical figures, Arthur and Merlin, both of whom are given a central place in his History' (Crick, 1992, p. 357). The legendary king of Britain, Arthur, and the enigmatic and sage-like magician, Merlin, emerge as central figures in the medieval literary tradition. Monmouth's position was viewed within the historiographical canon as initially ambiguous and is why John Spence states: 'Geoffrey of Monmouth's account of the legendary history of Britain was received sceptically by English historians but was nevertheless incorporated into the mainstream of historical writing in later medieval England' (Spence, 2013, p. 72).

In the early modern period, a different kind of writing emerged as illustrated in John Stow's *The Summarie of Englyshe Chronicles, The Chronicles of England*, and *The Annales of England* from 1565. 'John Stow was one of the best historians of that age; indefatigable in the trouble he took, thorough and conscientious, accurate—above all things devoted to truth—unlike our television historians today' (Rowse, 1971, p. 15). J. L. Rowse's critique from the early 1970s is as much a commentary on the way history was presented in his own time as that of Stowe's sixteenth-century England. Over a decade after Stow's account, Raphael Holinshed's *Chronicles of England, Scotland, and Ireland*, known as *Holinshed's Chronicles* (1577 and 1587), was published. In the nineteenth century, scholars identified that William Shakespeare drew in 13 of his plays on the 1587 version which is why it is 'often referred to as "Shakespeare's Holinshed"' (Story Donno, 1987, p. 229). An interesting exposition of Holinshed's work is provided by Igor Djordjevic who states that while it is 'historically distorted to some modern historians because of the presence of obviously fictional elements in the text, [...] its "poetic" truth is remarkably close to the "historical" truth about the people, events, and culture reconstructed by recent historical scholarship' (Djordjevic, 2010, p. 3).

The seventeenth-century histories that followed include Edward Hyde, First Earl of Clarendon's *The History of the Rebellion and Civil Wars in England*, which was completed after his fall from royal favour in 1667. Writing about his own troubled time may have made him didactic and, so, approaches his work as 'a moral act, designed to teach succeeding generations the truth about the English Civil War, or, as he thought of it, the Rebellion' (Hammond, 2023, p. 111). The later eighteenth-century historians were increasingly influenced by the broader ideas of the Enlightenment and began to see themselves as playing a role in this change. 'Historians were prominent among the architects of British power from the eighteenth century until very recently, as both policymakers and advisors to other policymakers; the rule of historians coincided with imperialism' (Satia, 2020, pp. 1–2). The top-down model that ensued in the nineteenth century included among its writers, aristocrats come politicians come historians. The Whig politician Thomas Babington Macaulay's *The History of England from the Accession of James the Second* commonly known as *The History of England* was published 1849–1861. The five-volume work focuses on 1688–1702, the period during and from the Glorious Revolution, that in doing so, contributes to the grand narrative, as Catherine Hall asserts: 'It told of the making of the nation, providing a master narrative of descent, defining who belonged and who was outside. Macaulay's story followed in many respects that of previous Whig historians, for it celebrated England's balanced constitution and its traditions of protecting the freedom of the subject and guaranteeing rights of property' (Hall, 2009, p. 506).

A further aristocrat come politician come historian in the twentieth century was the Conservative politician, Sir Winston Churchill. *A History of the English-Speaking Peoples* (1956–1958) saw the first of the four volumes being published the year after he stepped down as Prime Minister. Churchill's history was different from the histories that were being published in post-war Britain. What spurred on the new wave of writing was because 'after the Second World War there were great expectations that British society could be changed fundamentally for the better' (Fieldhouse, 2013, p. 25). The new Labour government headed by Clement Attlee heralded a move to nationalisation and the public sector that saw it take a greater role in the state and society. E. P. Thompson launched the Marxist journal *The New Reasoner* in 1957, which merged to form the *New Left Review* in 1960 and wrote his seminal critique *The Making of the English Working Class* (1963). The New Left attracted other Marxist writers of English and British history including Christopher Hill who was for a time a member of the Communist party, as had been E. P. Thompon. A lone wolf was Geoffrey Elton, an admirer of Churchill and later Margaret Thatcher who was 'combative' of Marxist history, arguing it provided a distorted interpretation of the past (Munro, 2015, p. 807). What these combined histories shared, was the same cause-and-effect determinist model of 'deep-lying forces which conform to fixed, though perhaps not always known, patterns of development' (Nagel, 1960, p. 291).

In the determinist model, historians do not engage in chaos theory whose complex systems are unpredictable. The past and the present are, however, chaotic systems and are not cleanly delineated where one ends and the other begins. A further issue is concerning the relationship between the past and history. J. H. Plumb argues there is 'a sharp distinction between the past and history' (Plumb, 2004, p. 11). Despite this being the case, even historians sometimes use the words the past and history to mean the same thing, as John Lukacs states: 'In most languages "history" has a double meaning. It is the past, but it is also the study of and description of the past, storytelling of a particular kind' (Lukacs, 2011, p. 1). The point is history is so subsumed within the dominant narrative that it is seen as the past. The underlying issue remains that history negates the role that subjectivity plays in this process. 'Historians bring their own memories to bear both on the choice of subjects they study and on the character judgments they make about human behaviour' (Winter, 2010, p. 12). While it would be impossible for historians not to be influenced by their own opinions, they are still presumed to be objective in the history they produce. What is important, that Michel de Certeau identifies, is that: 'Historians do not make histories, they can only engage in the making of histories' (de Certeau, 1988, p. 8).

The issues arising from these histories is addressed by Michel Foucault who in questioning the orthodoxy of history states that it imposes 'stable structures' where he believes there are none (Foucault, 2002, p. 6). Those that questioned the old orthodoxy shared the same ideological position, as Anna Clark, Stefan Berger, Marnie Hughes-Warrington, and Stuart Macintyre assert: 'In the 1960s, many historians were influenced by the New Left and by a left-wing politics that could take different shapes and include diverse ideological commitments' (Clark et al., 2018, p. 500). These ideological commitments were arguably less diverse than has been suggested in promoting a Marxist agenda. What did happen was that a friction was created between the old and the new which led to 'a tension between readings that unite and those that divide' (Black, 2015, pp. ix–x). Why this is important is because history should not be an instruction, but should be open to debate, in order to widen understanding and knowledge.

## HISTORICISING THE NATION

Since the post-war period, while there were competing viewpoints in historical writing, equally polarising positions were taken in architecture. Responding to the changing plethora of architectural styles from the nineteenth to the twentieth centuries, Joseph Rykwert adds: 'And then came modern' (Rykwert, 1990, p. 113). The roots of Modernism began with the Industrial Revolution, and as the world changed, so did the way of thinking about it. What had been accepted as industrial advancement, was viewed differently by the mid-twentieth century. Denis Rodwell states how 'the negative imagery of the nineteenth century industrial city in England and France, as portrayed in literature (including the novels of Charles Dickens and Emile Zola) and the visual arts (notably the engravings of London and Paris by Gustav Doré) [...] acted as the drivers for mainstream urban planning across much of the postwar Western world' (Rodwell, 2010, pp. 4–5). While much has been claimed about the destruction of historic British cities from German Luftwaffe bombing, they also suffered considerable damage from the modernising aims of the British post-war Conservative governments up to 1964 and the Labour governments from 1964 to 1970. During the first Harold Macmillan Conservative government, The Victorian Society was formed in 1958, as a 'charity dedicated to fighting for our Victorian and Edwardian heritage' (The Victorian Society (2024) https://www.victorian.society.org.uk/).

A major battleground was the Victorian railway station. The enemy was British Rail because of its proposed programme of modernisation. The sites included Philip Hardwick's Euston Railway Station (1837) and the Euston Doric Arch (1837) which 'were swept away in 1960–61 in the interests of modernity, despite widespread protest' (Cherry & Pevsner, 2002, p. 361). After the demolition of Euston, the nearby St Pancras Railway Station and the Midland Grand St Pancras Hotel (known as the Midland Grand Hotel) were next due for demolition. Despite the aesthetic value of the hotel's façade, 'with its imposing red brick, stone, and granite exterior' the move demonstrated how much had changed from the 1860s to the 1960s (Donnellan, 2022, p. 69). When the St Pancras site was originally developed, it was heralded for its architecture and engineering and for being 'the finest terminus in the world' (Anonymous, 1869, p. 376). The 1960s British Rail planners saw these Victorian buildings in a different light. What supported the Midland Grand Hotel and St Pancras Railway Station's case was that 'it was clear that demolition would repeat the Euston Arch furore for the benefit of British Rail alone' (Davis, 2022, p. 193). The demolition plans were abandoned. The buildings were awarded the protective Grade I listed heritage status in 1967.

A key campaigner was the writer and founding member of The Victorian Society Sir John Betjeman whose literary writing engages with an 'Arcadian Englishness' (Joyce, 2014, p. 56). Betjeman was interested as much in his own history, as wider history. While he added heft to the campaign, as an establishment figure, and went onto become the Poet Laureate from 1972, he did not alleviate the immediate problem of regenerating the St Pancras site. The hotel building in a much modified form did not reopen until 2011. In the late 1980s, Michael Jenner lamented the loss of 'London's most amazing display of High Victorian Gothic architecture' because the building had receded into the grime of the King's Cross skyline (Jenner, 1988, p. 189). At the time Jenner was writing, the idea that heritage could play an active role in reviving the built environment was changing. Margaret Thatcher's third Conservative government had already begun to see heritage less as a burden to the public purse and more as an economic driver. An example of this was the redevelopment of the Victorian Albert Dock in Liverpool from 1981 which was part of the Merseyside Development Corporation's programme of regeneration. From this point with the decline in manufacturing and shift to the service-based sector, what else was born was 'the "heritage industry"' (Hewison, 1987, p. 9). During the Thatcher decade, other ways of reappropriating the past were being deployed which reflected a renewed interest in 'especially things English' (Lowenthal, 1985, p. 6).

## Nostalgising the Past and the Post-War Country House Novel

The first wave of things English emerged from the early to mid-part of the twentieth century, when 'media representations of Britain, empire, and Commonwealth were Anglocentric' (Webster, 2005, p. 17). In the post-war period, these Anglocentric representations emerged through the country house novel. The earlier country house novels including Jane Austen's *Mansfield Park* (1814) engaged with themes of identity and class where the Anglocentrism is the assumed natural order of things. In the post-war country house novel, the Anglocentrism is a central feature of the narrative. The reason is that the post-war country house novel was about the end of the *English* rather than the British Empire. For this reason, the English characters sit in old English drawing rooms on old English settees surrounded by old English paintings of old family members, in even older English houses. What is represented is the fading legacy of a lost world and is why Katherine C. Henderson asserts: 'The rhetoric of historicity, preservation, and national homogeneity did not coalesce to form a sustained incorporation of an English—rather than British—identity within the "Great House" until the decline of Empire *and* of the country house' (Henderson, 2015, p. 94).

Post-Empire, Evelyn Waugh's *Brideshead Revisited: The Sacred and Profane Memories of Captain Charles Ryder* (1945) begins with Ryder an army captain in wartime Britain who finds himself garrisoned at Brideshead Castle in Wiltshire. Here he reflects on his earlier time as an Oxford University student and visits Brideshead with his friend and possible lover, the upper-class Sebastian Flyte. For the older Ryder, Brideshead no longer holds its 'delusive charm' (Heath, 1982, p. 202). While Brideshead may be 'one of the queerest novels of its time,' the narrative is underpinned by its Englishness, class, place, history, and nostalgia (Lockerd, 2018, p. 239). A further aspect of Brideshead is that it 'is a privileged embodiment of tradition in that it has been built with the stones of a castle previously existing in the valley it now commands' (Fernández, 2022, p. 88). Another post-war country house novel that harks back to a bygone age is

L. P. Hartley's *The Go-Between* (1953), which begins with the iconic open-ing sentence: 'The past is a foreign country they do things differently there' (Hartley, 1953, p. 9). With its tea and cucumber sandwiches, and croquet on the lawn, *The Go-Between* evokes a sepia-tinted, top-down vision of late Victorian England. For the wealthy family living in the large country house, they become the custodians of their past. In this most eponymous of settings, the country house represents an anatomy of 'social relationships' within its interior spaces in contrast to those of the outside world (Lefebvre, 1991, p. 27). In the wake of World War II, the country house novel offered certainty and the hope that the future would be the same.

The next time the country house novel had a major resurgence was in 1980s Thatcherite Britain. The Granada Television series *Brideshead Revisited* was broadcast on the ITV network in 1981. The distinctive voice of the actor Jeremy Irons playing the role of Ryder, the 'nostalgic narra-tor' took hold of the nation and contributed to the series accolades which endured for decades after its initial screening (Schweizer, 2005, p. 254). During this period, the Conservative government remained wedded to the idea of the nation's imperial past. The television adaptation shows Ryder, sketching Brideshead as if recording an old relic from the imperial past. Bernard Schweizer discusses what has been lost from this past. 'Ironically, Waugh's imagination (and hence, his income) thrived on the universal decline he lamented. *Brideshead* contains a shrewd meditation on that very paradox. Waugh's stand-in, the narrator Charles Ryder, makes a fortune by painting country houses before they are torn down' (Schweizer, 2005, p. 264). What remains at the root of the television adaptation and the novel is a picture of the past. 'In spite of having served as an icon of national preservation—indeed, perhaps precisely because it does so—the English country house takes on particular significance in fic-tion' (Henderson, 2017, p. 715). Further book dramatisations that shared the same themes of English (British) spaces which were not country house novels include other Granada Television produced series for the ITV network.

*The Jewel in the Crown* (1984) was based on Paul Scott's *Raj Quartet* novels (1965), which Florence Cabaret describes 'as one of the most criti-cal representations of the presence of Great Britain in India in the 1940s' that dually 'projects a nostalgic and melancholy gaze over a lost empire' (Cabaret, 2012, pp. 110 & 111). What is evident for Scott who had been a commissioned British officer in India is that 'the legacy of colonial life haunted him' (Qureshi, 2017, p. 61). Scott sets his story in the fictional Indian city of Mayapore in the final days of the British Raj in India. As Richard Dyer identifies, 'the processes of imperialism call forth white identities' and because of this there is nothing unusual about the British inhabitants treating the Indians as foreigners in their own city (Dyer, 1996, p. 225). Where this is demonstrated is through the spaces of the Indian city. Here, the British inhabit their private grand bungalows and work in their grand public government buildings. These places are in stark contrast to the noisy and threatening exterior world of India. David Dunn identifies how the television series 'used locations in India which were seldom on the well trodden paths of travelogues, but served rather to contrast the Otherness of the dirt and press of life in the bazaars and back streets of the Indian districts with the ordered calm of the Civil Lines' (Dunn, 2015, p. 43). *The Jewel in the Crown* foremost, represents us, civil, safe, and British, and them, dangerous, foreign, and other.

What is important in all histories, whether personal and anecdotal, or official and public, is what is written out. Avery F. Gordon reminds us: 'Perceiving the lost subjects of history—the missing and lost ones and the blind fields they inhabit—makes all the difference to any project trying to find the address of the present' (Gordon, 2008, p. 195). In 1950s and 1980s Britain, this was about searching for something that could not be found in the address of the present and alluded to that thing which never happened, but they (we) wished it had. Why else would the acclaimed historian and geographer David Lowenthal use the opening words from *The Go-Between* for his scholarly work *The Past is a Foreign Country* (1985)? What adds to the idea of the past being a foreign country is that the story takes place over a hot summer despite being set in England. On this point Jonathan Jones proposes: 'Grey skies and rain lie at the heart of English identity.' Jones intimates that this weather is part of the English psyche and because of this in the novel the relentlessly sunny days serve 'to evoke distance and memory, never the close proximity of modern life' (Jones, 2016, p. 1). What the weather contributes to is the *mise-en-scène* in *The Go-Between*, in turning the past into something mythic. The question is: is this any different from academic writing in separating the past from the present? The issue is that we are still looking at the past as if looking into the bottom of an old jam jar and is why Jerome de Groot asserts it 'is something indistinct, smoky, something that recalibrates the now in undefined ways and provokes anxiety and distress' (de Groot, 2016, p. 112). The underlining issue that Dennis W. Harding identifies is that 'the past seldom speaks for itself' but how can it otherwise? (Harding, 2020, p. 2). The question remains: should it be left to history alone to officially narrate the past?

The point is that history, for all its forensic analysis, is only an imagining of what was and is why Alison Landsberg asserts: 'All written history—even that written by academic historians—is inherently narrative, carefully plotted, fundamentally an imaginative construction on the part of the historian' (Landsberg, 2015, p. 11). De Certeau earlier proposed something darker concerning its ideological basis 'in remaining a narrative, historiography retains this "element of grandeur" that once characterised religion. In effect, narrative means impossible totalization' (de Certeau, 1988, p. 346). Through being colonised by history, this gives the appearance of resurrecting the past when, in fact, the reverse is true. 'Inhabited by the uncanniness that it seeks, history imposes its law upon the faraway places that it conquers when it fosters the illusion that is bringing them back to life' (de Certeau, 1988, p. 36). Historiography in fostering the illusion that it is resurrecting the past, needs to change. Lucien Hölscher argues for a new virtual historiography 'that goes beyond factual events to consider the possible alternative interpretations of the course of history without entering the field of counterfactual history' (Hölscher, 2022, p. 27). In extending beyond the notional and the tangible, the new historiography could draw on Herodotus in deploying the figurative and from the Anglo-Saxon histories for the legendary without fear of being cancelled for not maintaining the rigour of the historical canon. Crucially, the new historiography does not need to proceed towards a destination nor impose its own destiny on the past, and nor declare an alliance to a political party because history is not meant to dictate but to illuminate. What is important in the new historiography is that while historians can engage in the making of history, they must not engage in the making of the past.

REFERENCES

Anonymous. (1869). The Great St. *Pancras Railway Station. Scientific American,* 21(24), 376–376. https://doi.org/10.1038/scientificamerican12111869-376
Barthes, R. (1977). *Image Music Text* (S. Smith, Trans.). Fontana Press.
Benjamin, W. (2015). *Illuminations* (H. Zorn, Trans.). Penguin Random House (Imprint: The Bodley Head).

Black, J. (2015). *Clio's Battles: Historiography in Practice*. Indiana University Press.

Burrow, J. (2008). Herodotus: The Great Invasion and The Historian's Task. *The Yale Review*, *96*(1), 1–19. https://doi.org/10.1111/j.1467-9736.2008. 00355.x

Cabaret, F. (2012). Representations of Power Shifts Between Great Britain and India in *The Jewel in the Crown* (ITV, 1984). *TV/Series*, *2*(2), 110–127. https://doi.org/10.4000/tvseries.1403

Cherry, B., & Pevsner, N. (2002). *London 4: North*. Yale University Press.

Clark, A., Berger, S., Hughes-Warrington, M., & Macintyre, S. (2018). What Is History? *Historiography Roundtable. Rethinking History*, *22*(4), 500–524. https://doi.org/10.1080/13642529.2018.1528046

Cochrane, C. N. (1929). *Thucydides and the Science of History*. Oxford University Press.

Crick, J. (1992). Geoffrey of Monmouth, Prophecy and History. *Journal of Medieval History*, *18*(4), 357–371. https://doi.org/10.1016/0304-4181(92) 90008-M

Davis, J. (2022). *Waterloo Sunrise: London from the Sixties to Thatcher*. Princeton University Press. https://doi.org/10.1515/9780691220581

de Beauvoir, S. (2018). *The Ethics of Ambiguity* (B. Frechtman, Trans.). Open Road.

de Certeau, M. (1988). *The Writing of History* (T. Conley, Trans.). Columbia University Press.

de Groot, J. (2016). *Remaking History: The Past in Contemporary Historical Fictions*. Routledge. https://doi.org/10.4324/9781315693392

Djordjevic, I. (2010). *Holinshed's Nation: Ideals, Memory, and Practical Policy in the Chronicles*. Routledge. https://doi.org/10.4324/9781315586960

Donnellan, C. (2022). Building the Historic Environment—Values and Uses—Urban Regeneration at King's Cross Central, London. In M. S. de Waal, I. Rosetti, M. de Groot, & U. Jinadasa (Eds.), *Living (World) Heritage Cities: Opportunities, Challenges, and Future Perspectives of People-centered Approaches in Dynamic Historic Urban Landscapes* (pp. 67–74). Sidestone Press.

Dunn, D. (2015). A Passage to Manchester: Space, Place and Aesthetic in *The Jewel in the Crown*. *Critical Studies in Television*, *10*(3), 37–52. https://doi. org/10.7227/CST.10.3.4

Dyer, R. (1996). 'There's nothing I can do! Nothing!': Femininity, Seriality and Whiteness in *The Jewel in the Crown*. *Screen*, *37*(3), 225–239.

Evans, J. A. S. (1968). Father of History or Father of Lies; The Reputation of Herodotus. *The Classical Journal*, *64*(1), 11–17.

Fernández, C. S. (2022). Evelyn Waugh's Brideshead Revisited: Sites of Memory and Tradition. *Miscelánea: A Journal of English and American Studies*, *65*, 87–103. https://doi.org/10.26754/ojs_misc/mj.20226848

Fieldhouse, R. (2013). Thompson: The Adult Educator. In R. Fieldhouse & R. Taylor (Eds.), *E* (pp. 25–47). Manchester University Press.

Foucault, M. (2002). *The Archaeology of Knowledge and The Discourse on Language* (A. M. Sheridan Smith, Trans.). Routledge.

Gordon, A. F. (2008). *Ghostly Matters: Haunting and the Sociological Imagination*. University of Minnesota Press.

Gunn, V. (2009). *Bede's Historiae: Genre, Rhetoric and the Construction of Anglo-Saxon Church History*. The Boydell Press.

Hall, C. (2009). Macaulay's Nation. *Victorian Studies, 51*(3), 505–523.

Hammond, P. (2023). Clarendon's Moral History. *The. Seventeenth Century, 38*(1), 111–130. https://doi.org/10.1080/0268117X.2022.2115539

Harding, D. W. (2020). *Rewriting History: Changing Perceptions of the Archaeological Past*. Oxford University Press. https://doi.org/10.1080/0268117X.2022.2115539

Hartley, L. P. (1953). *The Go-Between*. Hamish Hamilton.

Heath, J. (1982). *The Picturesque Castle: Evelyn Waugh and his Writing*. McGill-Queens University Press.

Henderson, K. C. (2015). Claims of Heritage: Restoring the English Country House in Wide Sargasso Sea. *Journal of Modern Literature, 38*(4), 93–109. https://doi.org/10.2979/jmodelite.38.4.93

Henderson, K. C. (2017). New Britain, Old England: Heritage Renewed in Atonement. *MFS Modern Fiction Studies, 63*(4), 714–736. https://doi.org/10.1353/mfs.2017.0054

Herodotus. (2003). *The Histories* (A. de Sélincourt, Trans.) (revised ed.). Penguin Books.

Hewison, R. (1987). *The Heritage Industry: Britain in a Climate of Decline.* .

Hölscher, L. (2013). Mysteries of Historical Order: Ruptures, Simultaneity and the Relationship of the Past, the Present and the Future. In C. Lorenz & B. Bevernage (Eds.), *Breaking Up Time: Negotiating the Borders between Present, Past and Future* (pp. 134–151). Vandenhoeck & Ruprecht. https://doi.org/10.13109/9783666310461.134

Hölscher, L. (2022). Virtual Historiography: Opening History towards the Future. *History and Theory, 61*(1), 27–42. https://doi.org/10.1111/hith.12247

Hughes-Warrington, M. (2019). *History as Wonder: Beginning with Historiography*. Routledge.

Jenner, M. (1988). *London Heritage: The Changing Style of a City*. Michael Joseph.

Jones, J. (2016). Strangers in the World of the Emotions: Re-evaluating L.P. Hartley's The Go-Between. *WLA: War, Literature & the Arts, 28*, 1–12.

Joyce, H. (2014). "Behind the Backs of Houses": Landscapes of Englishness in the Postwar Railway Poetry of John Betjeman and Philip Larkin. *Transfers, 4*(2), 49–67. https://doi.org/10.3167/trans.2014.040205

Landsberg, A. (2015). *Engaging the Past: Mass Culture and the Production of Historical Knowledge.* Columbia University Press. https://doi.org/10.7312/land16574

Lateiner, D. (1990). Deceptions and Delusions in Herodotus. *Classical Antiquity, 9*(2), 230–246.

Lefebvre, H. (1991). *The Production of Space* (D. Nicholson-Smith, Trans.). Blackwell Publishing.

Lockerd, M. B. (2018). Decadent Arcadias, Wild(e) Conversions, and Queer Celibacies. *Brideshead Revisited. MFS Modern Fiction Studies, 64*(2), 239–263. https://doi.org/10.1353/mfs.2018.0019

Lowenthal, D. (1985). *The Past is a Foreign Country.* Cambridge University Press.

Lukacs, J. (2011). *The Future of History. Yale University Press.*. https://doi.org/10.12987/9780300175134

Munro, D. (2015). Michael Turnbull, G. R. Elton, and the Making of the Practice of History. *The Historical Journal, 58*(3), 805–825.

Nagel, E. (1960). Determinism in History. *Philosophy and Phenomenological Research, 20*(3), 291–317. https://doi.org/10.2307/2105051

Pelling, C. (2019). *Herodotus and the Question Why.* University of Texas Press. https://doi.org/10.7560/318324

Plumb, J. H. (2004). *The Death of the Past.* Palgrave Macmillan.

Qureshi, B. (2017). The Original Brexit: Rediscovering. *The Jewel in the Crown. Film Quarterly, 71*(1), 59–64.

Rodwell, D. (2010). Urban Conservation in the 1960s and 1970s: A European Overview. *Architectural Heritage, 21*(1), 1–18. https://doi.org/10.3366/arch.2011.0002

Rowse, A. L. (1971). John Stow as an Historian: A Commemoration Address. *Transactions of the London and Middlesex Archaeological Society, 23*(1), 15–18.

Rykwert, J. (1990). Book Review of Damie Stillman (1988) *English Neo-Classical Architecture. Eighteenth-Century Studies, 24*(1), 113–117. https://doi.org/10.2307/2738989

Satia, P. (2020). *Time's Monster: How History Makes History.* The Belknap Press of Harvard University Press.

Schiffman, Z. S. (2011). *The Birth of the Past.* Johns Hopkins University Press. https://doi.org/10.1524/hzhz.2013.0105

Schweizer, B. (2005). Evelyn Waugh's Brideshead Revisited and Other Late Novels. In B. W. Shaffer (Ed.), *A Companion to the British and Irish Novel, 1945–2000* (pp. 254–265). Blackwell Publishing.

Spence, J. (2013). *Reimagining History in Anglo-Norman Prose Chronicles* (Imprint: Boydell & Brewer Ltd). York Medieval Press.

Story Donno, E. (1987). Some Aspects of Shakespeare's "Holinshed". *Huntington Library Quarterly, 50*(3), 229–248.

The Victorian Society. (2024). The Victorian Society: Campaigning for Victorian and Edwardian Architecture. https://www.victoriansociety.org.uk/
Webster, W. (2005). *Englishness and Empire, 1939–1965*. Oxford University Press.
Winter, J. (2010). The Performance of the Past: Memory, History, Identity. In K. Tilmans, F. van Vree, & J. M. Winter (Eds.), *Performing the Past: Memory, History and Identity in Modern Europe* (pp. 11–34). Amsterdam University Press. https://doi.org/10.1515/9789048512027

## CHAPTER 3

# Whitehall: Places of History and State Spaces

**Abstract** Under King Henry VIII a Tudor court and executive council was established in 1530 at Whitehall Palace in London. The later Stuart court of King James I demonstrated a renewed belief in the Divine Right of Kings. By the end of the century, James I's dynastic intentions took a different course when King William III and Queen Mary II became a constitutional monarchy. The new Stuart vision was less about God and more about expanding the nation. When Whitehall Palace burned down the Stuart court never returned. In its place a new type of state emerged at Whitehall which was no longer tied to the idea of monarchy. Further major developments were underway in the opening decade of the eighteenth century through the creation of the United Kingdom of Great Britain. The constant in these events was Whitehall which by the nineteenth century was at the nexus of a global Empire. What ran Whitehall was the powerful bureaucracy of the Civil Service that continues to be run by its permanent and non-political civil servants. Post-Empire, and despite Britain's changing fortunes, an imperial rhetoric continued to pervade the spaces of Whitehall. When things changed was during a Black Lives Matter protest in 2020. The street action opened the debate concerning Britain and its history, and raised the questions: does this history need to be changed, can it be changed, and should it be changed?

**Keywords** Britain • Whitehall • Empire • Imperialism • Power • Identity

C. Donnellan, *British Contested History*, https://doi.org/10.1007/978-3-031-62209-0_3

## Introduction: The Palace of Whitehall

At the hub of the British Government is Whitehall whose historic environment dates to 1245 when the Archbishop of York, Walter de Grey, established York Place. The site was rebuilt in 1514 and turned into a grander
Palace for Cardinal Thomas Wolsey. By late 1529, it was in the possession
of King Henry VIII who remodelled it into the Palace of Whitehall and
made it his main London residence. A Banqueting House was added to
the site (Cox & Norman, 1930, p. 116). During Queen Elizabeth I's
reign temporary Banqueting Houses were constructed in 1572 and 1581
to receive foreign dignitaries (Department of the Environment, 1983,
p. 2). When the last one burned down in 1607 during the reign of King
James I, he commissioned a replacement to be built which was again
destroyed by fire in 1619. A new Palladian-style Banqueting House
opened in 1622 which still stands today. Further works to Whitehall Palace
were later commissioned by King Charles II and King James II. When a
fire damaged older apartments in 1691, it remained the largest palace in
Europe, the scale of which is addressed by Simon Thurley: 'Whitehall was
indeed the largest royal Palace in Europe: it covered twenty–three acres
compared with Versailles' seven and a half, the Escorial's eight and a half,
and Hampton Court's modest six' (Thurley, 1998, p. 47).

When Whitehall Palace burned down in 1698, it was not rebuilt. The
sole major building to survive was the Banqueting House. While the court
moved to St James's Palace, the state remained at the burned-out site of
Whitehall Palace which is why 'the cabinet office of today is housed in the
remains of the cockpit buildings [...]' (Thurley, 1998, p. 52). What
emerged was the 'political formation' of the state (Pearson, 1982, p. 1).
While the rest of the Whitehall site was allocated for residential leasehold
use, it 'remained under the control of the Crown' (Learmouth, 2021,
p. 362). The seventeenth-century Stuart and eighteenth-century Georgian
residences were replaced in the nineteenth century by public state buildings, which saw Whitehall emerge as the centre of an 'imperial administration' (Port, 1995, p. 274). Post-Empire the same vision continued to
resonate through Whitehall's historic environment. The point when this
began to be questioned was due to a Black Lives Matter demonstration in
2020 which highlighted the role that 'urban dynamics' plays in 'political
and social transformations' (Davis & Libertun de Duren, 2011, p. 5). The
reason that this is important is because Whitehall is more than a collection
of government buildings—it is the home of the British state. This chapter

looks at how and why Whitehall developed in the way it did and considers is there another way to endow it with new meanings and memories.

## THE SPACES OF THE DIVINE RIGHT OF KINGS

Henry VIII was the last monarch to live at Westminster Palace, and from there moved to York Place which he turned it into Whitehall Palace. While Whitehall Palace dually functioned as the place of his executive council, Westminster Palace remained 'the normal meeting place of Parliament' (Thurley, 1998, p. 48). What Whitehall Palace provided was the context to reflect Henry's ambitions which culminated in the Act of Supremacy (1534), that severed ties with the Papacy and the Church of Rome. The artist Hans Holbein the Younger painted, the since-destroyed, *Whitehall Mural* (1536–1537) on the wall of the Privy Chamber. An ink and water-colour cartoon (underdrawing) exists which depicts the left-hand section of the original painting showing Henry VIII and Henry VII. A smaller version by Remigius van Leemput from 1667 includes Jane Seymour, and Elizabeth of York on the right-hand side of the painting. What is notable as with the rest of Holbein's post-Reformation images is the 'huge physical presence' of Henry VIII (Howard, 1995, p. 65). The four figures are facing forward, standing around a stone tablet with a Latin inscription which ends on the line: 'The arrogance of the Popes has yielded to unerring virtue, and while Henry VIII holds the scepter in his hand religion is restored and during his reign the doctrines of God have begun to be held in his honour' (Foister, 2006, p. 94). The words endorsed Henry's belief in the Divine Right of Kings which during the English Reformation was given 'a new lease of life' (Burgess, 1992, p. 841).

The Divine Right of Kings was next enacted at the Stuart court at the Banqueting House through the court masque, 'a peculiar manifestation of courtly behaviour, of which the ceremonial and the ritual were vital components' (Demaubus, 2003, p. 299). On the Christian festival of Twelfth Night, 6 January 1605, James I and his Queen Consort, Anne of Denmark, attended the Banqueting House to participate in *The Masque of Blackness* (1605). Written by Ben Jonson, the performance featured Anne and her court ladies appearing in blackface makeup who 'with black dispaire' waited to be cleansed of their blackness by the King whose light was compared to the sun (Jonson, 2007, p. 9). The desire to cleanse their black skin by making it white was about, as Mary Floyd-Wilson asserts, 'the formation of racial identity' and about creating difference

(Floyd-Wilson, 1998, p. 186). The performance alluded to the monarch in having God-like powers. The spectacle of the masque was heightened by the setting of the Banqueting House, and while 'place does not have power,' it does for those who are invested in the idea of it being so (Sack, 1993, p. 327). While the Masque was a private court affair, it 'indirectly reached the public sphere by going into print' and so, its intentions were disseminated to a wider audience (Edgecombe, 2008, p. 31). James I's aim was to assert his authority which he did through increasingly public displays of power.

At the Banqueting House, 21 March 1610, James I gave a speech to Parliament in which he declared: 'The state of monarchy is the supremest thing upon earth; for kings are not only God's lieutenants upon earth, and sit upon God's throne, but even by God himself they are called gods' (The National Archives, 2024, https://www.nationalarchives.gov.uk/education/resources/james-i/divine-right/). When the Banqueting House burned down, a new Palladian-style building to designs by Inigo Jones opened in 1622. Three years later, James I was dead. King Charles I shared the same belief system as his father. 'Charles thought purely in terms of descending authority, never in terms of ascending authority and [...] tried to make the court a microcosm of what he wanted the larger microcosm of his kingdom to be—an ordered and virtuous commonwealth under his paternal rule' (Young, 1997, p. 81). Charles I believed in the 'body politic' in which, as the King, he had a temporal (physical) body and a political (metaphorical) body (Kantorowicz, 2016, p. 314). As the King, Charles I was the head of the body politic (the realm) and the state (the polity). A demonstration of this was when he 'governed the country without recourse to parliament' which later became known as the Personal Rule of Charles I from 1629 to 1640 (Brice, 1994, p. 110). Dissolving Parliament had a precedent, as 'the Stuart kings could and did refuse to call Parliament for long periods' however, what was unusual about this occasion is that it played a fundamental role in the English Civil War (Cox, 2012, p. 569).

The King's vision was further reflected in Sir Peter Paul Rubens and Studio's *The Apotheosis of James I* (c. 1632–1634). The paintings were installed in 1636 to the ceiling of the Banqueting House. The main central oval painting depicts James I at the point where he is to be taken up from earth to God. 'The King, with one foot on an eagle and the other on the imperial globe, is about to be raised to the heavens by the female figure of Justice as the reward for his earthly labours' (Royal Collection Trust, 2024, https://www.rct.uk/collection/408414/

the-apotheosis-of-james-i). The image echoes the tenets of James I's speech to Parliament in the older Banqueting House when he declared that God himself called him one of the gods. While the Personal Rule of Charles ended in 1640, 'his God-given rights led to conflict with Parliament and the Civil War of 1642–1649' (Jones, 2005, p. 11). During this period images of Charles I were withdrawn from public and private view, which included Hubert Le Sueur's equestrian *Statue of Charles I* (c. 1630–1633). The bronze statue had earlier been commissioned by the Lord Treasurer Richard Weston for the garden of his house at Roehampton. The culmination of events saw Charles I tried for High Treason against the state. The paradox was that Charles believed he was the state. For this reason, he 'clung to a vision of sacred kingship, in which his subjects owed their monarch obedience, service, and love' (Cressy, 2015, p. 7).

The question his trial raised was: who was the state? Was it the King, or was it Parliament? Parliament prevailed with its 'unshakeable certainty that God had a plan for England' (Polizzotto, 2016, p. 33). Charles I was found guilty and beheaded on scaffolding in front of the Banqueting House, 30 January 1649. The regicide was a bloody physical and a symbolic act in severing the head of the body politic. 'The king was executed, the House of Lords abolished, the Commonwealth of England proclaimed' (Skinner, 1974, p. 79). The Interregnum from 1649 until 1660 heralded a new era. The republic was run by Parliament with Oliver Cromwell at its helm. In 1653, he became the Lord Protector of the Commonwealth of England, Scotland, and Ireland and moved into the Cockpit within the Palace of Whitehall. The dilemma for Cromwell was that 'he searched for a parliament that would promote his vision of a godly commonwealth, and always it eluded him' (Smith, 2007, p. 14). The year after being made Lord Protector Cromwell moved into the royal apartments that had been earlier occupied by Charles I. When Cromwell died in 1658 at Whitehall Palace, so did his 'dictatorship' (Dillon, 2007, p. 10). He was succeeded by his son Richard who was unable to secure the support he required and stepped down from office which ended the protectorate.

The restoration of the monarchy in 1660 saw King Charles II dating his reign, from 30 January 1649, and because of this, he reigned 'in the shadow of his father's scaffold' (Ollard, 2000, p. 21). Whitehall Palace became his London residence, from where he decided to execute the people responsible for his father's death. Along with Cromwell was his son-in-law Henry Ireton, a General in the Parliamentary Army, and John

Bradshaw, the President of the High Court who tried Charles I. The men were, however, already dead. 'On Saturday, 26 January 1661, the tombs of Ireton, Cromwell and Bradshaw, which lay in the chapel of Henry VII in Westminster Abbey, were broken open in time for the anniversary of the regicide' (Farr, 2006, p. 3). Their corpses were taken to the place of execution for traitors, Tyburn, where they were hanged. Their heads were placed on spikes above Westminster Hall and their bodies thrown into common graves. Measures were also taken to restore Charles I's reputation. The *Statue of Charles I* was instated on the island south of Trafalgar Square (then the King's horses exercise yard) facing Whitehall, the place of his execution. The statue was positioned in a conspicuous place because Charles II was aware of political displays of power, as was his father. 'Charles had been conscious of sculpture, both as decoration for palace and garden and as a vehicle for propaganda, for the promotion of what today is called a "public image"' (Avery, 1980–1982, p. 136).

On Charles II's death in 1685, he was succeeded by his younger brother King James II who created new apartments at Whitehall Palace for his Queen, Anne Hyde, which included at the Holbein Gate 'a new Roman Catholic chapel. It was this latter building that was to contribute to the downfall of James' (Thurley, 2024, https://www.royalpalaces.com/palaces/whitehall-palace/). After James II was deposed during the Glorious Revolution of 1688, William of Orange and his wife Mary née Stuart accepted The Bill of Rights (1689) as a 'precondition for their enthronement' (Rowley & Wu, 2014, p. 103). William III and Mary II were no longer answerable to God but were to Parliament. With their dislike of Whitehall Palace, they relocated to Nottingham House (now Kensington Palace) and to Hampton Court Palace.

When William III and Mary II left Whitehall Palace, it ceased to be a royal residence. After it burned down in 1698, what was left at Whitehall was the political formation of a separate state. Along with an 'expanding state bureaucracy' what else grew was the Stuart expansionist vision which begun with James I in Ireland and the Plantation of Ulster in 1609 (Pettigrew, 2007, p. 9). Under William III the Stuart vision focused again on Ireland. The Battle of the Boyne (1690) was, however, 'only a partial success' (Troost, 2016, p. 280). To finance his military campaigns, the Bank of England was created in 1694 to fund the expansion of the Royal Navy and is why Geoffrey Elton states: 'The century of wars also made the fortunes of the Royal Navy' (Elton, 1992, p. 175). At the hub of these activities was the state bureaucracy of Whitehall which enabled the late

Stuart's vision to come to fruition under Queen Anne. The reason is outlined by Alan I. Macinnes: 'England had insufficient manpower to fight
war in Europe and America, to sustain domestic manufacturing and
expand Empire. Scotland was a ready reservoir' (Macinnes, 2023,
pp. 106–107). The mechanism for creating this vision was the Acts of
Union (1707), which formed the political bond between England and
Scotland that led to the United Kingdom of Great Britain.

## BUILDING THE EMPIRE—BUILDING WHITEHALL

The Hanoverian monarch King George I oversaw the creation of the
office of the Prime Minister when in 1721, Robert Walpole, first Earl of
Orford became the First Lord of the Treasury. King George II provided a
gift of a site of three houses which merged to become No. 10 Downing
Street, off Whitehall in 1732. A section of the Horse Guards Parade was
converted into a garden for Downing Street which was 'laid out and
developed at the expense of the State' (Minney, 1963, p. 46). King George
III in 1782 oversaw the new office of the Secretary of State for Foreign
Affairs who was appointed to headquarters in Cleveland Row behind
Downing Street. 'Between 1780 and 1815 Britain acquired extensive new
colonial territories. Some were the spoils of victory, others had been taken
for immediate or longer-term strategic purposes during the French wars,
or, as in the Indian subcontinent, to secure the internal stability necessary
to protect Britain's interests' (Laidlaw, 2005, p. 39). To meet the demands
of the expanding government office, a vast building complex was designed
by Sir George Gilbert Scott in the 'High Victorian' neo-classical style
which was under construction from 1861 to 1868 (Bradley & Pevsner,
2003, p, 266). The building on King Charles Street off Whitehall was
housed in four separate departments: the Foreign Office, the India Office,
the Colonial Office, and the Home Office. With its vast doorways, façades,
and decorations what it communicated and continues to be communicated is a rhetoric of power.

Further demonstrations of Whitehall's power are represented through its
historic statues. On King Charles Street facing St James's Park is John
Tweed's, bronze statue *Robert Clive* (1912). Commonly known as Clive of
India, he was the first British Governor of the Bengal Presidency. While he
died in 1774, the statue was made in the early twentieth century due to
George Nathaniel Curzon, first Marquess Curzon of Kedleston. Lord
Curzon was another imperialist who celebrated Clive for his contributions

to the British Empire. The statue also contributed to the idea of Clive as a British hero. 'Newspaper articles, official and unofficial histories, novels, photography, and film: they all helped to transform Clive into a personalised site of memory—shared by Britons and Indians and contested for two and a half centuries' (Goebelt, 2015, pp. 136–137). Clive's contested history is also the nation's contested history, due to his involvement with the British East India Company. Along with other European chartered trading companies, it was involved 'in purchasing, owning and trafficking Indian slaves in the seventeenth and eighteenth centuries' (Major, 2012, p. 49). The reason why Clive courted a range of public opinion was not because of his exploits in India but due to his alleged profiteering and is why 'he had to wait a long time for a national memorial' (Matthews, 2012, p. 24).

The position of Clive's statue in front of the Foreign Office acts as a testament of the imperial vision. What else is a testament to that vision is the Foreign Office's statuary designed by Henry Hugh Armstead and John Birnie Philip. Many of the sculpted images are of those who were involved with some form of geographical and colonial activity. As Edward W. Said asserts, 'Imperialism after all is an act of geographical violence through which virtually every space in the world is explored, charted, and finally brought under control' (Said, 1994, p. 225). The Whitehall Wing was originally occupied by the Home and Colonial Offices. The first floor-sculpted spandrels represent America, Australasia, Africa, Asia, and Europe which had been British dominions, and/or places of colonial exchange. The second-storey roundels include images of Britons who contributed to the advancement of Britain through usually some form of colonial or imperialist activities. They include Sir Frances Drake who circumnavigated the globe in a single expedition between 1577 and 1580 during the reign of Queen Elizabeth I who is also included in the sculptural scheme. It was on her behalf that Drake 'constituted the first assertion of English sovereignty on North American soil bordering on the Pacific Ocean' (Gough, 1992, p. 22). While Drake was a sea captain, explorer, and a slave trader, he contributed to 'Britain's seafaring prowess, as it moved from the colonial aspirations of the 17th century to the 19th-century expansion of empire' (Bradley, 2017, p. 3).

A further British explorer represented in the second-storey roundels is Captain James Cook (1728–1779) who undertook expeditions to the coasts of Canada and conducted three expeditions to the Pacific Ocean. These voyages were about discovery, territory, and British place-making. 'It was Cook's voyages in the 1770s and the subsequent convergence of

British, Spanish, Russian, French, and US commercial ventures along the American coastline that linked these parts of the Pacific to the rest of the ocean and beyond' (Igler, 2013, p. 9). Alongside Cook is the Scottish physician David Livingstone (1813–1873). While Livingstone was anti-slavery, he was also a Christian missionary, imperial reformer, explorer, and advocate of British interests in Africa. Andrew C. Ross outlines the esteem in which he was held in Britain during his lifetime, which contributed to the idea of 'the iconic Livingstone, patron saint of imperialism and the ideal Protestant missionary' (Ross, 2002, p. 240). An earlier Briton, who was also anti-slavery, and is represented in the roundels is William Wilberforce (1759–1833). Wilberforce spent from 1787 fighting to abolish the slave trade, but faced major opposition because 'the House of Commons voted to refer the issue to the colonial legislatures, which had no interest in even considering the case for abolition' (Short, 2009, p. 80). Wilberforce's perseverance led the Slave Trade Act in 1807. What his and the other statues represent is a conflicted vision of Britain.

## A Place of Remembrance

Along Whitehall on an island in the middle of the road by what is today is the Foreign, Commonwealth and Development Office is Edwin Lutyens's *The Cenotaph* (meaning empty tomb) (1919–1920). Originally, a temporary Cenotaph stood on the same site. Due to public demand, it was replaced with a permanent Portland stone memorial and unveiled on Armistice Day, 11 November 1920. When the Treaty of Peace between the Allied and Associated Powers and Germany was signed, 28 June 1919, a Victory Parade was planned in London. 'The Cenotaph was only one of several temporary structures along the parade route and played only a brief part in the celebrations, but somehow it caught the veterans' and public's imagination, an understated, abstract expression of the nation's grief' (Jones, 2005, p. 61). At the same time, 'the Cenotaph and the Tomb of the Unknown Soldier were conceived as imperial memorials' (Macleod, 2013, p. 647). At the centre of the memorials is Whitehall whose imperial rhetoric remains evident throughout its buildings. Henri Lefebvre proposes that these kinds of spaces act as 'the connections between national spaces of this kind and the world market, imperialism and its strategies' (Lefebvre, 1991, p. 112). Within this world market, Britain forged its imperial fortune. While Britain had been at the centre of this world market through the Empire, the conundrum is that it was seen as 'something that was judged to have happened overseas; although originating in Britain, imperialism remained marginal to the lives of most British people' (Thompson, 2011, p. 2).

The other reality was that Britain did not have the military capacity to manage its developing assets and is why Martin Pugh states: 'There was an element of illusion in this mid-Victorian triumphalism. In geographical terms Britain was the smallest of the Great Powers. With an army that was quite inadequate for the defence of her imperial possessions' (Pugh, 1999, p. 3). Britain in 1913, however, was controlling 23% of the world's population, and despite being geographically small, by 1920 covered approximately 24% of the planet's total land area. The location of its power base was Whitehall. After the Empire, the area including the Foreign Office and the Commonwealth Office continued to operate for a time as a symbol of 'national prestige' (Edwards, 1964, p. 471). While Whitehall was no longer at the heart of the Empire in the late twentieth century, its history was entrenched in its urban fabric. By the start of the twenty-first century Whitehall had also become subsumed into the historic environment, which was seen by the government as 'an asset of enormous cultural, social, economic and environmental value' (HM Government, 2010, p. 1). In doing so, Whitehall further signalled that it was rooted in the past, which made it appear more detached, and not quite part of modern Britain.

## State Spaces: Whitehall 2020—Black Lives Matter

During the weekend of 6–7 June 2020, Black Lives Matter (BLM) assembled in Trafalgar Square to march down Whitehall and into Parliament Square to express their views to the British Government inside the Houses of Parliament. The demonstration was one of several protests held simultaneously across British cities, in response to the killing of George Floyd, a black male by Derek Chauvin, a white Minneapolis Police Officer. The incident hit a nerve in British society concerning racism and its colonial past which opened the debate between society and the state in representing 'the forces of oppression' (Bernstein, 2005, p. 49). What the BLM action represented was the public sphere of 'private people gathered together as a public and articulating the needs of society with the state' (Habermas, 1989, p. 176). A splinter BLM initiative saw one activist attempting to torch the flag of the United Kingdom attached to the Cenotaph. Other actions included defacing the statue of Ivor

Roberts-Jones's *Sir Winston Churchill* (1973) in Parliament Square, which was sprayed with writing that accused the former Prime Minister of being a racist.

In Bristol, the BLM protestors pulled down John Cassidy's bronze memorial statue of *Edward Colston* (1875), who was a merchant, parliamentarian, and slave trader. Colston joined the Royal African Company which monopolised the British slave trade. He died in 1721. The statue was erected 125 years later in 1895, and as stated by Jessica Moody what this statue and others like it represent are 'the attitudes, anxieties and contexts of the times in which they were created' (Moody, 2021, p. 5). For the Bristol protestors Colston represented the worst kind of racism and is why they threw his statue into the river Avon. What followed the action was a spate of other statues of people who had slavery links being daubed with paint or removed in protest over 'the fiercely contested physical spaces of civic memorialisation across the Global North' (Price & Lea, 2024, p. 12). Petitions were launched elsewhere to remove other statues of those connected with the slave trade. Eva Branscome observes how 'far too many statues and other artefacts within the urban realm carry troubling histories, even if their contentious associations might have been forgotten. Acting as quasi-Trojan horses, they can appear benign enough within their cultural landscapes while yet silently continuing to reinforce socio-economic inequalities' (Branscome, 2021, p. 1).

Responding to the London protests, the Conservative government's Secretary of State for the Home Office Department Priti Patel declared: 'There is no excuse for pelting flares at brave officers, throwing bikes at police horses, attempting to disrespect the Cenotaph or vandalising the statue of Winston Churchill, one of the greatest protectors of our freedoms who has ever lived. It is not for mobs to tear down statues and cause criminal damage in our streets, and it is not acceptable for thugs to racially abuse black police officers for doing their jobs' (UK Parliament Hansard, 2020, https://hansard.parliament.uk/commons/2020-06-08/debates/212DD2A6-B810-4FDE-B3BD-1642F5BA1E86/PublicOrder). What the protests represented were the bigger issues facing Britain concerning sovereignty, post imperialism, and racism. The question the action raised: should this history be expunged? A different way of looking at this past, and indeed, any past is posed by Rodney Harrison who frames it from the perspective of the present: 'What does it mean to live in amongst the spectral traces of the past, the heterogeneous piling up of historic materials in the present?' (Harrison, 2013, p. 3). It is this kind of question that needs to be asked along with the others that ask for change.

A further point to consider is that Whitehall is the home of the state, it is the instrument of the democratic process and is why Judith Kapferer asserts: 'State power and democratic process have always been inscribed in the material structures of urban contexts, particularly in the capital cities of powerful contemporary social formations such as the United Kingdom' (Kapferer, 2007, p. 68). Unchecked, state power and the idea of the democratic process can, however, create the idea that there is one history and one identity. Since the inception of Whitehall Palace, from Henry VIII's executive council the site has been about the state. By the late twentieth century the modern state had evolved into 'a set of practices, relations and forms of authority bound up with many aspects of daily life' (Pearson, 1982, p. 3). Since that time the state has shifted its authority in being bound up with all aspects of daily life. While Whitehall has become the interface between politics and society, fundamentally it is something more important than the government. When the government falls, Whitehall does not because the state exists in perpetuity.

Foremost, Whitehall is the interface between the past and the present. The question is therefore: can new conversations take place at Whitehall? If this is not possible, the debates may become entrenched conflicts that could lead to crises, and perhaps this is what is needed, as Matthew Seeger and Tomothy l. Sellnow assert: 'Crises are transformational at a personal, institutional, and societal level [...] they are among the most powerful forces of change' (Seeger & Sellnow, 2016, p. vii). Can Whitehall, which has itself undergone considerable change from a palace to a burned-out site to a set of practices, facilitate a new vision of Britain? Can the places of its histories and the architectures of its imperialism be reset with new stories and memories? If Britain is no longer a nation, with one history and one past, as the state must change, then so must the nation.

## REFERENCES

Avery, C. (1980–1982). Hubert le Sueur, The 'Unworthy Praxiteles' of King Charles I. *The Volume of the Walpole Society*, 48, 135–209.

Bernstein, M. (2005). Identity Politics. *Annual Review of Sociology*, 31(1), 47–74. https://doi.org/10.1146/annurev.soc.29.010202.100054

Bradley, S. (2017). Celebrity, Politics and Francis Drake. *History Today*, 67(3), 3–4.

Bradley, S., & Pevsner, N. (2003). *London 6: Westminster*. Yale University Press.

Branscome, E. (2021). Colston's Travels, or Should We Talk About Statues? *ARENA Journal of Architectural Research, 6*(1), 1–29. https://doi.org/10.5334/ajar.261

Brice, K. (1994). *The Early Stuarts 1603–1640.* Hodder & Stoughton.

Burgess, G. (1992). The Divine Right of Kings Reconsidered. *The English Historical Review, 107*(425), 837–861. https://doi.org/10.1093/ehr/CVII.CCCCXXV.837

Cox, G. W. (2012). Was the Glorious Revolution a Constitutional Watershed? *The Journal of Economic History, 72*(3), 567–600.

Cox, M. H., & Norman, P. (Eds.). (1930). *Survey of London: Volume 13, The Parish of St Margaret, Westminster, (Part II: Neighbourhood of Whitehall, Volume 1).* B. T. Batsford.

Cressy, D. (2015). *Charles I and the People of England.* Oxford University Press.

Davis, D. E., & Libertun de Duren, N. (2011). Identity Conflicts in the Urban Realm. In D. E. Davis & N. L. de Duren (Eds.), *Cities and Sovereignty: Identity Politics in Urban Spaces* (pp. 1–14). Indiana University Press.

Demaubus, T. (2003). Ritual, Ostension and the Divine in the Stuart Masque. *Literature and Theology, 17*(3), 298–313.

Department of the Environment. (1983). *The Banqueting House Whitehall.* Department of the Environment.

Dillon, P. (2007). *The Last Revolution: 1688 and the Creation of the Modern World.* Pimlico.

Edgecombe, R. S. (2008). The "Courtly Popular" Orient of Ben Jonson's Court Masques. *Cahiers Élisabéthains, 73*(1), 31–38. https://doi-org.ezproxy.bu.edu/10.7227/CE.73.1.5

Edwards, A. T. (1964). The Foreign Office and the Commonwealth Relations Office. *Official Architecture and Planning, 27*(4), 469–473.

Elton, G. (1992). *The English.* Blackwell Publishing.

Farr, D. (2006). *Henry Ireton and the English Revolution.* The Boydell Press.

Floyd-Wilson, M. (1998). Temperature, Temperance, and Racial Difference in Ben Jonson's "The Masque of Blackness". *English Literary Renaissance, 28*(2), 183–209.

Foister, S. (2006). *Holbein in England.* Tate Publishing.

Goebelt, R. (2015). The Memory of Lord Clive in Britain and Beyond: Imperial Hero and Villain. In D. Geppert & F. L. Müller (Eds.), *Sites of Imperial Memory: Commemorating Colonial Rule in the Nineteenth and Twentieth Centuries* (pp. 136–152). Manchester University Press. https://doi.org/10.7765/9781526111890.00016

Gough, B. M. (1992). *The Northwest Coast: British Navigation, Trade, and Discoveries to 1812.* University of British Columbia Press.

Habermas, J. (1989). *The Structural Transformation of the Public Sphere: An Inquiry into a Category of Bourgeois Society* (T. Burger, Trans.). Polity Press.

Harrison, R. (2013). *Heritage: Critical Approaches*. Routledge.

HM Government. (2010). *The Government's Statement on the Historic Environment*. Department, Culture, Media & Sport.

Howard, M. (1995). *The Tudor Image*. Tate Gallery.

Igler, D. (2013). *The Great Ocean: Pacific Worlds from Captain Cook to the Gold Rush*. Oxford University Press.

Jones, N. R. (2005). *Architecture of England, Scotland, and Wales*. Greenwood Press.

Jonson, B. (2007). *The Masque of Blackness. The Masque of Beauty*. Benediction Classics.

Kantorowicz, E. (2016). *The King's Two Bodies: A Study in Medieval Political Theology*. Princeton University Press. https://doi.org/10.1515/9781400880782-011

Kapferer, J. (2007). Constructing a Public Sphere: Materiality and Ideology. *Social Analysis, 51*(1), 68–85. https://doi.org/10.3167/sa.2007.510106

Laidlaw, Z. (2005). *Colonial Connections, 1815–45: Patronage, the Information Revolution and Colonial Government*. Manchester University Press.

Learmouth, J. (2021). Living Amid the Royal Ruins: Women and Property in Eighteenth-Century Whitehall. *Journal for Eighteenth-Century Studies, 44*(4), 361–381. https://doi.org/10.1111/1754-0208.12799

Lefebvre, H. (1991). *The Production of Space* (D. Nicholson-Smith, Trans.). Blackwell Publishing.

Macinnes, A. I. (2023). *A History of Scotland*. Bloomsbury Academic.

Macleod, J. (2013). Britishness and Commemoration: National Memorials to the First World War in Britain and Ireland. *Journal of Contemporary History, 48*(4), 647–665. https://doi.org/10.1177/0022009413493940

Major, A. (2012). *Slavery, Abolitionism and Empire in India, 1772–1843*. Liverpool University Press.

Matthews, P. (2012). *London's Statues and Monuments*. Shire Publications.

Minney, R. J. (1963). *No. 10 Downing Street, A House in History*. Little, Brown and Company.

Moody, J. (2021). Off the Pedestal: The Fall of Edward Colston. *Public History Review, 28*, 1–5. https://doi.org/10.5130/phrj.v28i0.7776

Ollard, R. (2000). *The Image of the King: Charles I and Charles II*. Phoenix Press.

Pearson, N. (1982). *The State and the Visual Arts: A Discussion of State Intervention in the Visual Arts in Britain, 1760–1981*. The Open University Press.

Pettigrew, W. A. (2007). Free to Enslave: Politics and the Escalation of Britain's Transatlantic Slave Trade, 1688–1714. *The William and Mary Quarterly, 64*(1), 3–38.

Polizzotto, C. (2016). Speaking Truth to Power: The Problem of Authority in the Whitehall Debates of 1648–9. *The English Historical Review, 131*(548), 31–63.

Port, M. H. (1995). *Imperial London: Civil Government Buildings in London 1851–1915*. Yale University Press.

Price, D., & Lea, S. (2024). *Entangled Pasts, 1768—Now: Art, Colonialism and Change*. In D. Price, E. Chadwick, C. Gilroy-Ware, & S. Lea (Eds.), *Entangled Pasts, 1768—Now: Art* (pp. 11–18). Colonialism and Change.

Pugh, M. (1999). *State and Society: A Social and Political History of Britain 1870–1997* (2nd ed.). Hodder Arnold.

Ross, A. C. (2002). *David Livingstone: Mission and Empire*. Hambledon & London.

Rowley, C. K., & Wu, B. (2014). *Britannia 1066–1884: From Medieval Absolutism to the Birth of Freedom under Constitutional Monarchy, Limited Suffrage, and the Rule of Law*. Springer.

Royal Collection Trust. (2024). https://www.rct.uk/collection/408414/the-apotheosis-of-james-i

Sack, R. D. (1993). The Power of Place and Space. *Geographical Review, 83*(3), 326–329. https://doi.org/10.2307/215735

Said, E. W. (1994). *Culture and Imperialism*. Vintage Books.

Seeger, M. W., & Sellnow, T. L. (2016). *Narratives of Crisis: Telling Stories of Ruin and Renewal*. Stanford University Press.

Short, E. (2009). William Wilberforce and the Fight for Life. *Human Life Review, 35*(3), 80–97.

Skinner, Q. (1974). Conquest and Consent: Thomas Hobbes and the Engagement Controversy. In G. E. Aylmer, ed., *The Interregnum: The Quest for Settlement 1646–1660* (revised ed., pp. 79–98). Macmillan.

Smith, D. L. (2007). Oliver Cromwell and the Protectorate Parliaments. In P. Little (Ed.), *The Cromwellian Protectorate* (pp. 14–31). The Boydell Press.

The National Archives. (2024). (James' I speech in the Banqueting House, Whitehall, 21 March 1610). https://www.nationalarchives.gov.uk/education/resources/james-i/divine-right/

Thompson, A. (2011). Introduction. In A. Thompson (Ed.), *Britain's Experience of Empire in the Twentieth Century* (pp. 1–32). Oxford University Press. https://doi.org/10.1093/acprof:oso/9780199236589.001.0001

Thurley, S. (1998). The Lost Palace of Whitehall. *History Today, 48*(1), 47–52.

Thurley, S. (2024). (Royal Palaces). https://www.royalpalaces.com/palaces/whitehall-palace/

Troost, W. (2016). *William III, the Stadholder-King: A Political Biography* (J. C. Grayson, Trans.). Routledge.

UK Parliament Hansard. (2020). (The Secretary of State for the Home Department). https://hansard.parliament.uk/commons/2020-06-08/debates/212DD2A6-B810-4FDE-B3BD-1642F5BA1E86/PublicOrder

Young, M. B. (1997). *Charles I*. Macmillan Press.

## CHAPTER 4

# Greece and Mesopotamia in Britain: Changing Places

**Abstract** This chapter examines how Britain's appetite for primacy extended to the appropriation of overseas' heritage when the Parthenon sculptures were removed from the Acropolis in Athens and installed in the British Museum in London where they have been on display since 1817. The following decade artefacts from Assyria were acquisitioned from a private collection, with greater numbers arriving directly from site excavations in the 1840s and 1850s. The Greek and Mesopotamian collections represented two different worlds. The former was revered as the cradle of Western European civilisation, while the latter from Mesopotamia, which today equates to modern Iraq, northeastern Syria, southeastern Turkey, and southwestern Iran, was seen as something foreign and other. What the British Museum contributed to were ideas of paternalism and entitlement, as well as issues of ownership and site displacement which has created a complex situation for a modern nation. The extent of this was demonstrated when the British Prime Minister Rishi Sunak was scheduled to meet the Greek Prime Minister Kyriakos Mitsotakis in November 2023, to discuss the Parthenon sculptures but cancelled, at the last minute, to avoid a confrontation. More often it is left to the British Museum to field these questions, which continues to assert it is a universal museum and that the sculptures will remain in its ownership, and therefore, in London. This chapter examines how this overseas heritage has become part of Britain's contested history and considers how these issues arising from its world collections might be resolved.

Keywords   British Museum • Greece • Mesopotamia • Archaeology •
Contested History • Material Heritage

## INTRODUCTION: CONTESTED HISTORY
## AND CRITICAL HERITAGE

Contested history begins when the past is 'organized into a story' (White, 1973, p. 5). The defining moments of these stories become watersheds in history. A notable watershed is the Golden Age of Athens, 480–404 BC. What it encompassed was the Athenian democracy and the Athenian empire which contributed to the image of the city as the political and cultural epicentre of the ancient world. Framing these events was the natural 'durable elevated platform' of the Acropolis (McGregor, 2014, p. 18). On top of the Acropolis remains its defining monument, the Parthenon (447 BC–432 BC) which over the passage of time attracted international admiration. In eighteenth-century Britain it was already held high esteem to the extent that in some quarters it was envied which resulted in a quantity of the Parthenon sculptures being taken by the Scottish aristocrat Thomas Bruce, seventh Lord Elgin. When they were shipped to Britain between 1801 and 1812, this was, therefore, not about the 'cultural patrimony of a defeated foe,' it was about British hegemony (Sandholtz, 2007, p. 1). Their removal was also not originally intended as an act of civic mindedness as the sculptures were taken by Elgin 'to decorate his estate in Scotland' (Lobell, 2009, p. 34). Making the sculptures public property happened when Elgin decided to sell them to the British Government. What has since ensued has been a difficult relationship with Greece which continues to dispute Britain's legal ownership of them and is why the UK's House of Commons continues to assert 'they were legitimately acquired' (Woodhouse & Pepin, 2017, p. 3).

The decade following the acquisition of the Parthenon sculptures, the British Museum acquired a private collection of antiquities from Assyria in Northern Mesopotamia. The excavations from the 1840s and 1850s by Austen Henry Layard greatly added to the collection when major Mesopotamian antiquities were shipped back to Britain. When they arrived, they became subsumed into the nation's own heritage, and because of this 'British national pride swelled with this archaeological and aesthetic conquest' (Stieber, 2003, p. 292). While Assyromania escalated this was not about Assyria, it was about the British imagination and its possession of this ancient culture. Despite the public's reaction, these acquisitions were not held in the same esteem as the Greek antiquities, which is why Magnus T. Bernhardsson asserts: 'Compared to the penultimate Greek sculptures from the Parthenon recently brought to the Museum, the artifacts from Mesopotamia were considered second-rate' (Bernhardsson, 2006, p. 44). This chapter examines how these different narratives emerged by addressing how these collections were acquired and how this has created a complicated colonial legacy for the nation. The question is: can this situation begin to be resolved?

## A Sense of Place: Athens

An unfinished temple on the Acropolis dedicated to Athena was sacked by the Persians in 480 BC, which served 'as a memorial to what had happened' (Boardman, 2000, p. 234). This changed when a new Parthenon was overseen by Pericles and is assumed to have been designed by Ictinus and Callicrates, with Pheidias responsible for the sculptural scheme. What they created became the embodiment of Athenian culture and a 'symbol of democracy' (Beard, 2010, p. 118). Below the Parthenon, the city of Athens, had at its core the agora, which functioned as a place for commercial, civic, social, and religious activities. The agora was also an assembly area for state affairs and the Athenian democracy which contributed to the idea of how: 'Imperial Athens became a model for the ancient world' (Evans, 2001, p. 212). After the city lost its position, the Parthenon survived as a temple dedicated to Athena for nearly 1000 years despite undergoing earthquakes, fire, wars, explosions, and looting. 'A Byzantine-style round-roofed apse at the east entrance' was also added, when it was also turned in Christian Church (St. Clair, 2022, p. 178). The Parthenon was also converted into an Islamic Mosque, and despite its many changes, it retained much of its sculpture until the eighteenth century. This changed when Elgin visited the site on his way to take up his role as the Ambassador at the Sublime Porte of Constantinople and shortly embarked on negotiations with the Ottoman authorities to remove the sculptures, as Greece was then under Ottoman rule.

At the same Elgin was appointed to the role of Ambassador in 1799, the Napoleonic campaign in Egypt was underway. The French officer Pierre François-Xavier Bouchard discovered the *Rosetta Stone* (196 BC). Before the *Rosetta Stone* was the *Rosetta Stone*, it was a fragment stele (slab) 'inscribed with a priestly degree—the Memphis

Degree—concerning the cult of King Ptolemy V Epiphanes (205–180 BC) in three ancient scripts, hieroglyphic, demotic and Greek' (Parkinson et al., 1999, p. 25). The stele was part of a larger slab that was possibly taken from a temple in the royal town of Sais that was later reused as building material in Fort Julien near the town of Rashid (Rosetta). Bouchard recognised the importance of the *Rosetta Stone* in possessing 'the key to the hieroglyphic script of dynastic Egypt' (Caygill, 2002, p. 19). The *Rosetta Stone* was in the possession of France until the Capitulation of Alexandria in 1801, when it became a British acquisition, and was moved to the British Museum. At the time it was taken from France, Elgin obtained a *firman* (permit) from the Ottoman authorities to initially remove the Parthenon sculptures which 'were in bad repair' (Parry, 2022, p. 47). The initial request developed into something more radical when 247 ft of the 524 ft of the Parthenon's frieze was taken along with 15 of the 92 metopes, 17 pediment figures, and various architectural details. The Erechtheion, the Propylaia, and the Temple of Athena Nike also had sculpture and architectural members removed.

The consequence of these actions was that it divested these sites of many of their intrinsic elements, and for those who lived there it severed their 'emotional and psychological engagement with [that] place' (Convery et al., 2012, p. 2). The loss was irrelevant to Elgin who removed them under the faint chivalric gesture of rescuing them from further destruction on the Acropolis and is why Fiona Rose-Greenland states: 'Athens was a shadow of its former self: it appeared to be a tumbledown of ruins and scattered inhabitations. In his mind, and in the mind of fellow travellers, the sculptures had no place in Greece. Britain—politically and economically strong, culturally sympathetic—was the heir apparent' (Rose-Greenland, 2013, p. 668). While Britain believed it was the heir apparent the effect of these 'dislocating processes' permanently impacted on the city's historic 'place-based' identity (Low, 2017, p. 1). In Britain not everyone approved of Elgin's actions, Lord George Gordon Byron condemned him for what he believed was akin to grand looting. While Lord Byron was regarded as a sympathiser for Greek independence from Ottoman Turkey, there were also those who considered Elgin's actions 'an abuse of his status as ambassador' (Woodhouse & Pepin, 2017, p. 7). There were others 'who justified his actions as interfering with nothing which was not already in ruins' (Woodhouse & Pepin, 2017, p. 7).

## THE PARTHENON SCULPTURES IN BRITAIN

When Elgin chose to sell the sculptures to the British Government, it set up a Parliamentary Select Committee Inquiry in 1816 to test the legitimacy of his legal ownership of them. During the Inquiry the sculptures were referred to as the Earl of Elgin's Collection, and, thereafter, as the Collection. (They became commonly known in Britain as the Elgin Marbles). The Select Committee raised four points therefore, relating to the Collection: (1) The authority which permitted its acquisition. (2) The circumstances under which it was obtained. (3) The artistic merit for making it public property for the purpose of promoting the study of the Fine Arts in Great Britain. (4) The financial value including the expenses incurred concerning its removal and transportation to England (House of Commons, 1816, p. 1). A group of British artists were also invited to submit their views about its aesthetic value who agreed it 'set an entirely new standard in ancient art' (St. Clair, 1998, p. 248). The outstanding acquisition for the British Museum was the large section of the Parthenon's frieze which was, and still is, considered to either represent the procession of the national festival of the Panathenaic commemorating the birth of Athena or a procession of the Panathenaic Games. Whatever scene is represented, they each relate to the history and heritage of Athens. The reason for them becoming internationally coveted was that their ancient Greek antecedence was seen 'as something belonging to the legendary sphere, to another time' (Hamilakis, 1999, p. 306).

The Parthenon was also regarded 'by many as the pinnacle of classical architecture' (Leitzel, 2022, p. 2). The sculpture and the building represented a conflation of ideas about the ancient city's past which was where the mythic met the real. For this reason, the Parthenon's West pediment sculptures represented the mythical contest between Athena and Poseidon for supremacy over the land of Attica. These fragments are now in the British Museum. Much of what remains of the East pediment sculpture which depicted the birth of Athena from the head of her father Zeus are also in the British Museum. Why the sculptures are important is because they represent 'some of the most remarkable pieces of ancient Greek art in existence' (Jenkins, 2016, p. 2). What underpins their importance is that they are 'bound to co-constructed myths and national narratives and (collective) memory' of Athens' past (Angouri et al., 2017, p. 216).

What the Parthenon sculptures in nineteenth-century Britain represented was the nation's growing imperial aspirations which dated to ancient Rome rather than Athens as it played a key role in England's early development when it was under Roman rule from 43 AD until 410 AD. Later British imperial vision echoed similar ideals in extending its economic power base outside of Britain. From the eighteenth century, Britain endeavoured to associate itself with ancient Rome and ancient Greece through architecture. The first British Museum at Montagu House was replaced by the larger purpose-built classical Greek Revival building with its Ionic edifice which completed in 1852. The Reading Room began construction in 1854 and looked to imperial Rome rather than Athens. With its massive domed ceiling it echoes the Pantheon in Rome. What the building and the reading room demonstrate is that 'classical antiquity played a pivotal role in British culture with two strains—Greece and Rome—jostling for ascendancy' (Fehlmann, 2007, p. 354). The Greco-Roman architectural style, as Carol Duncan asserts, 'could signal a firm adherence to Enlightenment values' (Duncan, 1995, p. 10). Amidst these values, the British Museum emerged as one of the Enlightenment's major proponents as a public museum presenting world histories, in an open and free public space.

The former Director of the British Museum, Neil MacGregor, declared: 'It is the only place in the world where you can see the cultures of the globe gathered together under a single roof' (MacGregor, 2004, p. 6). In celebrating the range of collections, including the Parthenon sculptures what he overlooked was how they were originally acquired. His reason for them remaining in London is a position that continues to be endorsed by the present trustees. 'The Acropolis Museum allows the Parthenon sculptures that are in Athens (about half of what survives from the ancient world) to be appreciated against the backdrop of Athenian history. The Parthenon sculptures in London are an important representation of ancient Athenian civilisation in the context of world history' (British Museum, 2024, https://www.britishmuseum.org/about-us/british-museum-story/contested-objects-collection/parthenon-sculptures/parthenon). The rationale for the British Museum retaining the sculptures and its other international collections is because it sees itself as 'a museum of the Enlightenment rather than the product of empire: a "Universal Museum" with an encyclopedic collection' (Beresford, 2015, p. 9). When the British Museum opened in 1759, it was created as a living encyclopaedia, in response to the publication of the *Encyclopédie* in France from

1751. The British Museum provided the physical embodiment of the *Encyclopédie* in a public space. 'The British Museum was thus a universal museum in every sense of the word—a true product and even embodiment of the Enlightenment, and certainly one of its greatest achievements' (Sloan, 2004, p. 14). How the British Museum became a universal museum was through its donations, gifts, and acquisitions from site excavations.

## Changing Places: Mesopotamia and Britain

The notable site excavations began in the 1840s in Mesopotamia. What led to the Mesopotamian excavations was the earlier bequest of Assyrian antiquities from Claudius James Rich. In his role as the British East India Company's Resident (diplomat) in Baghdad from 1808 to 1821, he was aware of the 'cartographic challenges' that surrounded him (Livingstone, 1992, p. 350). What Rich provides in his *Memoir on the ruins of Babylon* (1816) is neither a 'discovery' nor an 'interesting hypothesis' but a preliminary geographic survey of the land (Rich, 1816, p. 2). Twenty years later, he provides 'a general inspection of the remains of Nineveh' which was useful for the later British site excavations (Rich, 1836, p. 30). Additionally, the Assyrian antiquities he donated to the British Museum were instrumental in the embryonic development of this collection which is outlined by Nancy Stieber. 'These objects became the seed of the museum's stunning collection of Mesopotamian antiquities, which was further enriched by the sculpture excavated at Nimrud by Austen Henry Layard (1817–1894)' (Stieber, 2003, p. 292). In rejecting his life as a London lawyer Layard set off for a colonial posting in Ceylon (today Sri Lanka). Layard arrived in Mosul in 1840 and went onto Baghdad and Babylon, as well as Khuzistan and Luristan (Fales, 2017, p. 74).

During his travels Layard met the French vice-consul, Paul-Émile Botta, who shared an interest in the history of Mesopotamia. In the Ottoman capital Constantinople, Layard met Sir Stratford Canning, the British Ambassador to the Ottoman Empire who valued 'his enterprise, his intelligence, and his willingness to share his own conspiracy theories about Britain's many enemies in and beyond the city' (Parry, 2022, p. 268). Despite this Canning was unable to secure an appointment through the Foreign Office for Layard to work for him. Canning personally funded him, however, to return to Mosul from there he was able to visit Nimrud. 'A plea to Canning to support the excavation of Nimrud largely fell on deaf ears until Botta's major Assyrian discoveries made the news in late 1844. At this point, the pressure of Anglo-French diplomatic competition prevailed and Layard's wish was granted, albeit accompanied by a limited budget' (Fales, 2017, p. 74). At this point, archaeology was an embryonic science that enabled those without related knowledge, but the legitimacy of their home powers, to assume a defining role in its development. Layard's excavation work was to achieve several objectives, including the increase of a Western local presence (Parry, 2022, p. 268). The need for a Western, and specifically, a British and French, presence was not to quell the local people but was to counter imperial Russian directives through this part of Mesopotamia as a route into the Mediterranean and in the other direction to India.

The role of the archaeologist was, therefore, more than about recovering and analysing material culture, as demonstrated through the role of Layard: 'The public image of Layard as intrepid discoverer of the Assyrian capital of Nineveh was in fact generated within the extra-archaeological agendas of national power, institutional prestige and personal advancement' (Malley, 2004, p. 2). While Layard claimed he made the discovery, 'the ruins of Nineveh were discovered by Western travellers, most famously Carsten Niebuhr (1733–1815)' (Petit & Morandi Bonacossi, 2017, p. 20). During the Nineveh excavations, Layard was assisted by Hormuzd Rassam, a national born in Ottoman Mesopotamia, who worked at the excavations of Nimrud from 1845 to 1847, and Nineveh from 1849 to 1851. Rassam contributed to significant acquisitions being acquired by the British Museum. When the vast stone sculptures arrived, they received an enthusiastic public reception akin to the adulation given to a home coming, winning team. 'Importing Assyria into England' became a question of national pride (Malley, 2004, p. 2). For this reason, 'the Shipping of the Great Bull was treated as a national event by *The Illustrated London News* which entreated the government to fund Layard's patriotic work' (Malley, 1996, p. 154).

The antiquities excavated included several thousand fragments bearing the cuneiform script from the Royal Library, which were later identified as making up part of the twelve 12 incomplete Akkadian clay tablets depicting the *Epic of Gilgamesh* (c. 2100 BC–1200 BC). In nineteenth-century Britain, the *Epic of Gilgamesh* represented a strange and foreign land which was rooted in the idea of the Orient 'the place of Europe's greatest and richest and oldest colonies [...] and one of its deepest and most recurring images of the other' (Said, 1978, p. 9). Where it was disseminated was through the spaces of European literature and translations. 'Many popular sources on the archaeological rediscovery of Assyria in the nineteenth century begin with references to dreamy, childhood visions of the East, based on texts like *The Thousand and One Nights*' (Bohrer, 2003, p. 3). The Middle Eastern and South Asian stories were compiled during the eighth to thirteenth centuries. The first European version was translated into French through Antoine Galland's *Les Mille et une nuits, contes arabes traduits en français* (1704–1717). The stories include 'Aladdin's Lamp' and 'Ali Baba and the Forty Thieves,' which are not in the original Arabic manuscript. An anonymously translated version appeared in English from c. 1706 to 1721. A later English translation by Sir Richard Francis Burton *The Book of the Thousand Nights and One Night* (1885–1887) was published in 16 volumes. Burton's additional text includes notes that emphasise the sexual imagery in some of the stories. Collette Colligan outlines how the work 'was just one of many translations that he published through the Kama Shastra Society [...] with the primary purpose of publishing erotic and semi-erotic Indian and Arab texts' (Colligan, 2002, p. 31).

## Reconstructing Mesopotamia in the Early Twentieth Century

By the early twentieth century, Mesopotamia was attracting a stream of British and American visitors, when travelling was 'an act of conspicuous consumption, a new luxury for well-off members of the upper and middle classes' (Mairs & Muratov, 2015, p. 2). For many of the travellers what they went in search of they did not find, for others, they were more than compensated in their search for 'the place where Scheherazade's tales of *A Thousand and One Nights* had been set' (Atia, 2010, pp. 232–233). One of the travellers was the Oxford University graduate Gertrude Bell, who first visited Mesopotamia in 1909. On her return she documented, surveyed, mapped, and photographed the ancient sites, and as Lisa Cooper claims: 'Her photographs often provide, even to this day, an indispensable record of these monuments' (Cooper, 2017, p. 87). Bell became the first woman appointed to British military intelligence in 1915 and was awarded the rank of Major Miss Bell. She also supported the idea of an independent Arab nation but was 'in an uncomfortable position with regard to the Fertile Crescent' (Regeur, 2020, p. 6). The crescent-shaped region in the

Middle East included Mesopotamia that saw Britain assume interim control of the country which included its antiquities. 'Ostensibly, the ultimate aim was to prepare Iraq for independence. At the same time, this goal was to be achieved fully in line with British interests. Nowhere were these concerns more manifest than in archaeology' (Bernhardsson, 2006, p. 93).

At the Cairo Conference in 1921 territorial boundaries were the main question and for Britain it also addressed and 'how to cut the costs of occupying Mesopotamia' (Fromkin, 2001, p. 503). The attendees included Sir Winston Churchill, in his position as the Secretary of State for the Colonies, T. E. Lawrence (Lawrence of Arabia) as Special Advisor to the Colonial Office, and Bell who was the Oriental Secretary for the High Commissioner of Iraq. She was also instrumental in drawing the new borders for the map. Bell supported Prince Faisal when the Kingdom of Iraq was inaugurated in 1921. Faisal named Bell as the Director of Antiquities for the new Iraq Museum in 1924 'after she had convinced him of the need for a special law to preserve Iraq's archaeological treasures and to regulate excavations' (Allawi, 2014, p. 473). While the excavations were regulated, there was a conflict of interests. Bell was responsible for the guardianship of the antiquities and for the introduction of 'pair division of the findings between Iraq and the country that had sent the archaeological expeditions to Mesopotamia' (Lippolis, 2017, p. 321). The paradox was that Bell 'acted overtly as a political agent for the British Empire' yet was disapproved of by imperialists who wanted greater British control in Iraq (Bryce et al., 2013, p. 52).

When Britain's role in the formal administration of the Kingdom of Iraq ended in 1932, it continued to engage with its past. The renewed interest in archaeological excavations in 'the 1920s and 1930s changed the face of Near Eastern archaeology' (Lippolis & Messina, 2008, p. 7). One of the archaeologists was Max Mallowan, who married the crime writer Agatha Christie in 1930. Christie published *Murder in Mesopotamia* (1936), which revolves around an archaeological excavation at Tell Yarimjah near Hassanieh. It is based on the excavation site of Ur which Christie first visited in 1928 and where she later met Mallowan in 1930 (McCall, 2001, p. 40). The story is set four years before the book's publication in 1932 when the Kingdom of Iraq was in its final year of British administration. The shifting tides of colonialism provide the backdrop to this murder mystery. '*Murder in Mesopotamia* is notable for its exotic setting, the unusual murder and the depiction of an interesting and sharpy observed set of suspects' (Cholidis, 2001, p. 348). Supporting the main cast of suspects are the Iraqi nationals who veer from minor to serious criminals that conform to the idea of 'the colonial stereotype' (Roberts & Hackforth-Jones, 2005, p. 1). Christie's ideas about British ethnocentrism are made clear through how 'the large variety of Eastern peoples and customs coalesce into a distinct image' of the other (Schiffer, 2001, p. 303). While her books reached a wide audience, the question is: what kinds of ideas did her husband's work propagate about British archaeology in Mesopotamia?

## ARCHAEOLOGY AND A CONFLICTED PRESENT

The vision to create the British School of Archaeology in Iraq (BSAI) originated from Bell who in her will in 1926 left a donation for its establishment. The Colonial Office administrator in the Middle East, Sir Percy Cox with Bell's friends and associates founded the BSAI in 1932 (McCall, 2001, p. 157). The BSAI was funded by a British Government grant in 1946, which enabled it to establish a base in Baghdad. Mallowan was named its first director and remained throughout his tenure and after, keen to emphasise the BSAI's 'closest collaboration with the British Museum, thereby continuing a partnership which began with Layard in the middle of the last century' (Mallowan, 1966, p. 15). Mallowan remained the BSAI's director until 1961 and later became its chairman from 1966 until 1970, and president from 1970 until 1978. When the BSAI became the British Institute for the Study of Iraq (BISI) in 2007, it continued its archaeological excavations but with a shift in focus towards greater research and education. When things changed was with the United States-led invasion of Iraq.

The most shocking images were the scenes of violence and destruction of the nation's ancient heritage. 'In April 2003, the world watched in horror as part of Iraq's cultural heritage disintegrated among the rubble of Saddam Hussein's regime. [...] For those to whom Iraq meant only terror, weapons of mass destruction, or oil, several thousand years of history between the Tigris and the Euphrates opened into public view' (Nissen & Heine, 2009, p. vii.). The casualties included the Museum of Iraq and other museums and libraries around the nation that were looted and vandalised. A former Colonel of the United States Marine Corps Matthew Bogdanos who later led the repatriation of many of the objects raised the following questions: 'Was the looting the work of random opportunists or professional thieves? Was it an inside job? How much of the theft dated to 2003 and how much had taken place years, or perhaps even decades, earlier? [...] There were many questions and no answers' (Bogdanos, 2005, p. 482). One thing that was clear was that the world was reminded of Mesopotamia's ancient past. The oldest city in the Assyrian Empire was Nineveh, its settlement began circa 6000 BC. Athens was inhabited since circa 3000 BC, but it was not until 1400 BC that it became a centre of the Mycenaean civilisation. The Parthenon was built much later, from 447 BC. What the world saw televised was more than the toppling of Hussein's statue, it was the toppling of thousands of years of history and heritage.

The former Director General of Antiquities of Iraq Dr Donny George Youkhanna after the American invasion wrote: 'The very image of Iraq today is connected more than ever to its past' (George, 2006, p. 7). When the Iraq Museum reopened in 2015, many of the looted works were returned, but many were not. Concerning the Mesopotamian artefacts that were earlier acquired by Britain, these remain on display in the British Museum. The larger objects are exhibited on the ground floor in accessible areas, yet these objects still do not attract the same attention as the Parthenon sculptures. The reasons are because they originate from outside of Europe and because of the way they have been researched. Work on ancient Athens attracts researchers from the social sciences and the humanities with as many archaeologists and art historians researching this field. Research on Mesopotamia is largely through the social sciences, as Zainab Bahrani identifies: 'Archaeology, especially in the US has been more allied to the sciences, rather than the humanities, and visual representations and **iconographies** have been given far less attention in general books on Mesopotamia' (Bahrani, 2017, p. 13). For this reason and others, a conversation is to be had with Iraq over the British Museum's ownership of the Mesopotamian antiquities, on the basis that 'Mesopotamian archaeology as a modern discipline is rooted in the entrepreneurial and colonial past of the Western powers' (Matthews, 2003, p. 1).

The Parthenon sculptures continue to court the most controversy because they were acquired through a complex colonial narrative. A solution can only mean a compromise and at present there is no question of one. The Greek Ministry of Culture, 5 January 2023, issued the following statement. 'We repeat, once more, Greece's fixed position that it does not recognize the British Museum's right of possession, outright possession, and ownership of the sculptures, as they are a product of theft' (Orthodox Times, 2023, https://orthodoxtimes.com/ministry-of-culture-british-museum-has-no-legal-right-to-parthenon-sculptures-a-product-of-theft/). The British Museum Trustees were also resolute in their response.

'Successive Greek governments have refused to acknowledge the Trustees' title to the Parthenon Sculptures' (British Museum, 2023, https://www.britishmuseum.org/about-us/british-museum-story/contested-objects-collection/parthenon-sculptures). If the British Museum's ownership is not acknowledged, then a loan arrangement is not possible. Is the solution, therefore, to accept the present situation? One positive outcome is that the debate has extended beyond the walls of the museum. People who may not normally feel they have a stake in heritage are now voicing their opinions about these antiquities. Furthermore, the notoriety surrounding the Parthenon sculptures has even become a reason to visit the British Museum. The debate has also given a spotlight to the Acropolis Museum which opened in 2009. If the Parthenon sculptures are returned to Greece, they will be exhibited inside the Acropolis Museum and not returned to the Parthenon. Cost is also a consideration. At the time of writing, visits to the Parthenon are 30 Euros (for a combined ticket with other sites), exclusive private visits outside of normal hours for groups of up to five are 5000 euros.

What the Acropolis Museum offers (at a summer admission of 15 euros, the British Museum is free) is that it is in Athens, the home of the sculptures, and has, therefore, far greater proximity to their original site and can also provide natural light. James Beresford identifies how this 'is frequently offered as a key argument in favour of repatriating the Elgin Marbles to Athens, nonetheless, the best preserved of the sculptures—the Marbles that comprise the frieze—are poorly served by the illumination within the Museum' (Beresford, 2015, p. 24). While the British Museum does not have natural light that is effective or otherwise, it faces a litany of criticisms, some of which refers to it as being a monolithic institution and a place 'of dust, decay and neglect; of power and control' (Hooper-Greenhill, 2004, p. 556). Is there another argument that the British Museum which opened in 1759 has itself become a heritage site of the Enlightenment? Does the British Museum reflect the 'powerful analytical concepts and inspirational values of the Enlightenment to promote mutual understanding and respect amongst peoples, rather than use them as a teleological rationale for the inequalities of the status quo?' (O'Neill, 2004, p. 199). On this last point, the British Museum hosts world-class collections from Mesopotamia, and Greece and many more places outside of Britain, and as MacGregor states they are all under one roof. Is the British Museum, therefore, a valuable universal historical resource and heritage site that should be left as it is? Or is it a relic from the past and the site of contested history that needs to be dismantled?

REFERENCES

Allawi, A. A. (2014). *Faisal I of Iraq*. Yale University Press.

Angouri, J., Paraskevaidi, M., & Wodak, R. (2017). Discourses of Cultural Heritage in Times of Crisis: The Case of the Parthenon Marbles. *Journal of Sociolinguistics, 21*(2), 208–237. https://doi.org/10.1111/josl.12232

Atia, N. (2010). A Relic of Its Own Past: Mesopotamia in the British Imagination 1900–14. *Memory Studies, 3*(3), 232–241.

Bahrani, Z. (2017). *Mesopotamia: Ancient Art and Architecture*. Thames & Hudson.

Beard, M. (2010). *The Parthenon*. Profile Books.

Beresford, J. M. (2015). Museum of Light: The New Acropolis Museum and the Campaign to Repatriate the Elgin Marbles. *Architecture_MPS, 7*(1), 1–35. https://doi.org/10.14324/111.444.amps.2015v7i1.001

Bernhardsson, M. T. (2006). *Reclaiming a Plundered Past: Archaeology and Nation Building in Modern Iraq*. University of Texas Press.

Boardman, J. (2000). The Elgin Marbles: Matters of Fact and Opinion. *International Journal of Cultural Property, 9*(2), 233–262. https://doi.org/10.1017/s0940739100771074

Bogdanos, M. (2005). The Casualties of War: The Truth About the Iraq Museum. *American Journal of Archaeology, 109*(3), 477–526.

Bohrer, F. N. (2003). *Orientalism and Visual Culture: Imagining Mesopotamia in Nineteenth-Century Europe*. Cambridge University Press.

British Museum. (2023). (The Parthenon Sculptures). https://www.britishmuseum.org/about-us/british-museum-story/contested-objects-collection/parthenon-sculptures

British Museum. (2024). (The Parthenon Sculptures: The Trustees' statement). https://www.britishmuseum.org/about-us/british-museum-story/contested-objects-collection/parthenon-sculptures/parthenon

Bryce, D., MacLaren, A. C., & O'Gorman, K. D. (2013). Historicising Consumption: Orientalist Expectations of the Middle East. *Consumption Markets & Culture, 16*(1), 45–64. https://www.tandfonline.com/doi/full/10.1080/10253866.2012.662830

Caygill, M. (2002). *The Story of the British Museum* (3rd ed.). The British Museum Press.

Cholidis, N. (2001). "The Glamour of the East": Some Reflections on Agatha Christie's *Murder in Mesopotamia*. In C. Trümpler (Ed.), *Agatha Christie and Archaeology* (pp. 335–350). The British Museum Press.

Colligan, C. (2002). "Esoteric Pornography": Sir Richard Burton's Arabian Nights and the Origins of Pornography. *Victorian Review, 28*(2), 31–64. https://doi.org/10.1353/vcr.2002.0019

Convery, I., Corsane, G., & Davis, P. (2012). Introduction: Making Sense of Place. In I. Convery, G. Corsane, & P. Davis (Eds.), *Making Sense of Place: Multidisciplinary Perspectives* (pp. 1–8). The Boydell Press.

Cooper, L. (2017). Gertrude Bell and the Monuments of Nineveh. In L. P. Petit & D. Morandi Bonacossi (Eds.), *Nineveh, The Great City: Symbol of Beauty and Power* (pp. 87–90). Sidestone Press.

Duncan, C. (1995). *Civilizing Rituals: Inside Public Art Museums*. Routledge.

Evans, J. A. (2001). The Parthenon Marbles—Past and Future. *Contemporary Review, 279*(1629), 212–218.

Fales, F. M. (2017). Austen Henry Layard. In L. P. Petit & D. Morandi Bonacossi (Eds.), *Nineveh, The Great City: Symbol of Beauty and Power* (pp. 74–77). Sidestone Press.

Fehlmann, M. (2007). As Greek as It Gets: British Attempts to Recreate the Parthenon. *Rethinking History, 11*(3), 353–377. https://doi.org/10.1080/13642520701353256

Fromkin, D. (2001). *A Peace to End All Peace: The Fall of the Ottoman Empire and the Creation of the Modern Middle East* (Owl Books ed.). Henry Holt & Company.

George, D. (2006). Introduction. In G. Curatola (Ed.), *The Art and Architecture of Mesopotamia* (pp. 7–11). Abbeville Press Publishers.

Hamilakis, Y. (1999). Stories from Exile: Fragments from the Cultural Biography of the Parthenon (or 'Elgin') Marbles. *World Archaeology, 31*(2), 303–320. https://doi.org/10.1080/00438243.1999.9980448

Hooper-Greenhill, E. (2004). Changing Values in the Art Museum: Rethinking Communication and Learning. In B. M. Carbonell (Ed.), *Museum Studies: An Anthology of Contexts* (pp. 556–575). Blackwell Publishing.

House of Commons. (1816). *Report from the Select Committee of the House of Commons on the Earl of Elgin's Collection of Sculptured Marbles*. John Murray.

Jenkins, T. (2016). *Keeping Their Marbles: How the Treasures of the Past Ended up in Museums … and Why They Should Stay There*. Oxford University Press.

Leitzel, J. (2022). Athens or London? The Parthenon Marbles and Economic Efficiency. *Social Sciences & Humanities Open, 6*(1), 1–13. https://doi.org/10.1016/j.ssaho.2022.100325

Lippolis, C. (2017). The Iraq Museum in Baghdad. In L. P. Petit & D. Morandi Bonacossi (Eds.), *Nineveh, The Great City: Symbol of Beauty and Power* (pp. 321–323). Sidestone Press.

Lippolis, C., & Messina, V. (2008). Discoverers and Discovery of Mesopotamia. In R. Parapetti (Ed.), *Iraq Museum* (pp. 3–16). State Board of Antiquities and Heritage.

Livingstone, D. N. (1992). *The Geographical Tradition: Episodes in the History of a Contested Enterprise*. Blackwell Publishing.

Lobell, J. A. (2009). A New Home for Treasures of the Acropolis. *Archaeology*, *62*(5), 32–37.

Low, S. (2017). *Spatializing Culture: The Ethnography of Space and Place*. Routledge.

MacGregor, N. (2004). Preface. In K. Sloan (Ed.), *Enlightenment: Discovering the World in the Eighteenth Century* (pp. 6–7). The British Museum Press.

Mairs, R., & Muratov, M. (2015). *Archaeologists, Tourists, Interpreters: Exploring Egypt and the Near East in the Late 19th–Early 20th Centuries*. Bloomsbury Academic. https://doi.org/10.5040/9781474220309.ch-003

Malley, S. (1996). Austen Henry Layard and the Periodical Press: Middle Eastern Archaeology and the Excavation of Cultural Identity in Mid-Nineteenth Century Britain. *Victorian Review, 22*(2), 152–170. https://doi.org/10.1353/vcr.1996.0013

Malley, S. (2004). Shipping the Bull: Staging Assyria in the British Museum. *Nineteenth–Century Contexts, 26*(1), 1–27. https://doi.org/10.1080/08905490410001683273

Mallowan, M. E. L. (1966). *Nimrud and its Remains* (Vol. 1). Collins.

Matthews, R. (2003). *The Archaeology of Mesopotamia: Theories and Approaches*. Routledge.

McCall, H. (2001). *The Life of Max Mallowan: Archaeology and Agatha Christie*. The British Museum Press.

McGregor, J. H. S. (2014). *Athens*. The Belknap Press of Harvard University Press.

Nissen, H. J., & Heine, P. (2009). *From Mesopotamia to Iraq: A Concise History* (H. J. Nissen, Trans.). The University of Chicago Press.

O'Neill, M. (2004). Enlightenment Museums: Universal or Merely Global? *Museum and Society, 2*(3), 190–202.

Orthodox Times. (2023). (Ministry of Culture: British Museum has no legal right to Parthenon Sculptures, a product of theft). https://orthodoxtimes.com/ministry-of-culture-british-museum-has-no-legal-right-to-parthenon-sculptures-a-product-of-theft/

Parkinson, R., Diffie, B., Fischer, W., & Simpson, R. S. (1999). *Cracking Codes: The Rosetta Stone and Decipherment*. University of California Press.

Parry, J. (2022). *Promised Lands: The British and the Ottoman Middle East*. Princeton University Press. https://doi.org/10.1515/9780691231457

Petit, L. P., & Morandi Bonacossi, D. (2017). Nineveh, the Great City. Symbol of Beauty and Power. In L. P. Petit & D. Morandi Bonacossi (Eds.), *Nineveh, The Great City: Symbol of Beauty and Power* (pp. 15–22). Sidestone Press.

Regeur, S. (2020). *Winston S. Churchill and the Shaping of the Middle East, 1919–1922*. Academic Studies Press.

Rich, C. J. (1816). *Memoir on the Ruins of Babylon* (2nd ed.). Longman, Hurst, Rees, Orme, Brown & Murray.

Rich, C. J. (1836). *Narrative of a Residence in Koordistan: And on the Site of Ancient Nineveh; with Journal of A Voyage Down the Tigris to Bagdad and an Account of a Visit to Shirauz and Persepolis.* James Duncan.

Roberts, M., & Hackforth-Jones, J. (2005). Introduction: Visualizing Culture across the Edges of Empires. In J. Hackforth-Jones & M. Roberts (Eds.), *Edges of Empire: Orientalism and Visual Culture* (pp. 1–19). Blackwell Publishing. https://doi.org/10.1002/9780470773901

Rose-Greenland, F. (2013). The Parthenon Marbles as Icons of Nationalism in Nineteenth–Century Britain. *Nations and Nationalism, 19*(4), 654–673. https://doi.org/10.1111/nana.12039

Said, E. W. (1978). *Orientalism.* Routledge & Paul Kegan.

Sandholtz, W. (2007). *Prohibiting Plunder: How Norms Change. Oxford University Press.* https://doi.org/10.1093/acprof:oso/9780195337235.001.0001

Schiffer, R. (2001). Agatha's Arabs: Agatha Christies in the Tradition of British Oriental Travellers. In C. Trümpler (Ed.), *Agatha Christie and Archaeology* (pp. 303–333). The British Museum Press.

Sloan, K. (2004). "Aimed at Universality and Belonging to the Nation": The Enlightenment and the British Museum. In K. Sloan (Ed.), *Enlightenment: Discovering the World in the Eighteenth Century* (pp. 12–25). The British Museum Press.

St. Clair, W. (1998). *Lord Elgin and the Marbles* (3rd ed.). Oxford University Press. https://doi.org/10.1093/acprof:oso/9780192880536.001.0001

St. Clair, W. (2022). *The Classical Parthenon: Recovering the Strangeness of the Ancient World.* Open Book Publishers.

Stieber, N. (2003). Protecting Nimrud. *Journal of the Society of Architectural Historians, 62*(3), 292–293. https://doi.org/10.2307/3592515

White, H. (1973). *Metahistory: The Historical Imagination in Nineteenth–Century Europe.* The John Hopkins University Press.

Woodhouse, J., & Pepin, S. (2017). *The Parthenon Sculptures* (Briefing Paper No. 02075). House of Commons Library.

## CHAPTER 5

# Liverpool: The Spaces of Remembering and the Places of Forgetting Again

**Abstract** A charter was granted to Liverpool in 1695 by King William III, which provided the legislation to create a town council. The power invested in the council enabled it to build the world's first commercial wet dock which was under construction from 1709. Geographically, Liverpool benefitted from its location in northwest England on the eastern side of the Mersey Estuary, adjacent to the Irish Sea, and the Atlantic Ocean. The town was ideally located for transatlantic trade, which included the slave trade. An Act for the Abolition of the Slave Trade was passed in 1807. Slavery remained, however, legal in most of the British Empire until the Slavery Abolition Act was passed in 1833. The accumulation of Liverpool's various trading activities and subsequent need for expansion resulted in the later building of the Albert Dock. When it opened in 1846, it provided a mechanised and non-combustible dock and warehouse system. While the Albert Dock was heralded as a feat of industrial engineering, by the beginning of the twentieth century it had become obsolete. The site was awarded Grade I listed building status in 1952 and was subject to various planning proposals until it became the focus of a Conservative government initiative through the Merseyside Development Corporation in 1981. Renamed the Royal Albert Dock in 2018, the site today presents a more salubrious account of the city's past. This chapter examines the changing identity of the port of Liverpool and considers why it is important not to forget through the places of history but to remember through the spaces of the past.

**Keywords** Liverpool • Port city • Slave trade • Albert Dock • History
• Maritime heritage

INTRODUCTION: HAUNTED HISTORIES

Major epochs are built on contested histories which develop through forgetting, because memory 'can be impaired by selectively retrieving parts of
the same event' (Brown et al., 2012, p. 24). What is forgotten becomes
the 'spectrally troubled' because no matter how potent the exorcism, these
ghosts are never fully expelled (Frosh, 2013, p. 5). Edward S. Casey identifies 'the relationship between place and event' and 'the inherent spatiality
of history' (Casey, 2007, p. 507). In the case of Liverpool this relationship
was demonstrated through the place of the port, the event of the slave
trade, and the (haunted) spatial history shared by Britain, Africa, and the
Americas. By the 1750s, Liverpool had become the command-and-con-
trol centre for this enterprise in Britain. The engine room was the dock-
yards which emerged as 'the site of extensive shipbuilding for the slave
trade' (Morgan, 2007a, p. 19). The ships were then loaded with goods for
West Africa which were traded for slaves who were sent in ships to the
Americas. The ships that returned to Liverpool, carried 'goods such as
sugar, coffee, cocoa, cotton, tobacco and wood' (National Museums
Liverpool, 2024, https://www.liverpoolmuseums.org.uk/archivesheet3).
What supported these activities was the city's maritime infrastructure and
with its 'rising volume of shipping, Liverpool built six wet docks during
the eighteenth century. These were funded by the Liverpool Corporation
to a sum in excess of £1 million' (Morgan, 2007a, p. 18).

The maritime activities went in tandem with the city's expansion that
included the development of new streets for merchant's housing. These
were in stark contrast to the living conditions on board the slave ships,
which included The Brooks that was in operation from 1781 (Royal
Museums Greenwich, 2023, https://images.rmg.co.uk/asset/21421/).
The Liverpool slave ship was one of many that undertook the Middle
Passage, which was the enforced sea voyage for slaves from Africa to the
Americas and took six to eight weeks. In bad weather it could increase to
13 weeks or more. During the journey, the slaves remained below deck
with little room to move in. What bolstered the trade was industrialisation
through 'the growing availability of cheap, high-quality metals,' which
included copper sheathing and wrought iron for shipbuilding (Kelly et al.,

2021, p. 240). While the relationship between the Empire and the slave trade is recognised, the corresponding one with industrialisation is often overlooked. A further point is that Liverpool's City Council has been keen to rebrand itself as a modern city, through its new building developments, that in doing so, seemingly wishes to disengage with certain aspects of its past. This chapter addresses the questions—how did this history happen and how can what has been unremembered—be remembered?

## Maritime Liverpool

At the end of the seventeenth century in Liverpool there was 'a great upsurge of industrial and commercial activity' (Stephenson, 1955, p. 61). By the mid-eighteenth century, it had become 'the largest slave trading port city in Europe, whose ships transported more enslaved African people to the Americas than any other port city' (Moody, 2020, p. 7). Liverpool was not the only British Port engaged in this activity, Bristol led the way in the seventeenth century. The accumulation of Britain's slave-trading activities meant it dominated the trade between 1640 and 1807, and along with Portugal, accounted for approximately 70% of African slaves being transported to the Americas. A knock-on effect of the trade was that 'the reinvestment of proceeds gave stimulus to trading and industrial development throughout the north-west of England and the Midlands' (Shaw, 2020, p. 16). The generated revenue was considerable which saw the profits reflected in the city's new developments. 'With an emphasis on transformation and renewal, these changes in the urban landscape were related to notions of improvement and the creation of a civic identity' (McDade, 2012, p. 207). Where this was represented was in the new public buildings that included the town hall which was built between 1749 and 1754 to a design by John Wood the Elder. The private developments included the merchant's houses which were laid out 'on a formal Georgian grid' (Taylor & Davenport, 2009, p. 12).

The merchants quarter included the area adjacent to and north of Duke Street including Parr street, Seel Street, Fleet Street, Wood Street, Bold Street, and Slater Street. The area was named the RopeWalks after the long straight streets where rope making 'had been one of the earliest of Liverpool industries' (Muir, 2013, p. 223). Within Ropewalks is Parr Street. The Street takes its name from the banker and slave trader whose house and five-storey warehouse to the rear was built in 1799 on the corner site of Colquitt Street. His slave ship the *Parr* had berths for 700 slaves. Parr invested in at least 30 voyages for the ship. The greatest concentration of slave traders was clustered in houses along Hanover Street, which was 'favoured by the mercantile élite' (Earle, 2015, p. 145). North of Hanover Street is Tarleton Street named after the merchant family who included three generations of slave traders. A member of the last generation was Banastre Tarleton who became a Member of Parliament for Liverpool in 1790. He used his position in 'vociferously defending the slave trade, on which the fortunes of his own and other prominent Liverpool families had been founded' (Egerton, 1998, p. 220). Sir Joshua Reynolds's *Colonel Tarleton* (1782) hangs in the National Gallery, London, as John Bonehill asserts: 'Reynolds' portrait is one of absolute authority and martial command: a surety visualised through the surrounding "trophies" of enemy cannon and standards: the poised self-control of the officer in the midst of violent chaos: and the accentuation of the officer's corporeal presence' (Bonehill, 2008, p. 125). For the American Patriots, Banastre was 'the most feared officer in the British forces in America, as commander of the audacious British Legion' (Kostyal, 2013, p. 40).

What Tarleton reflected was the ideology of a colonising and subjugating nation. The antecedence for this began in the earlier period of mercantilism which promoted colonial interests through monopolising markets. What developed was a complex situation, as Christine Levecq states: 'The British had a long history of mercantilism and government intervention in matters of trade' (Levecq, 2008, p. 96). Mercantilism also established the transatlantic slave trade, and because it did not take place on British shores, there was the case in Britain that it was out of sight and out of mind. How the slave trade was facilitated was by seeing the slaves as something other. This colonial vision was conceived through a belief system that existed in 'the truly chaotic world of *collective consciousness*,' which in this instance was the collective British mind (Jung, 2001, p. 137). From the 1770s, the British abolitionist movement gathered momentum which was supported by a growing section of society who vehemently disapproved and found it 'morally distasteful' (Morgan, 2007b, p. 150). The Abolition of the Slave Trade Act (1807) ended the buying and selling of enslaved people within the British Empire but did not protect those already enslaved. Many enslavers continued to trade illegally. Under Captain Hugh Crow, the last British slaver ship sailed from Liverpool the year the Act was passed. The Slavery Abolition Act (1833) legally ended slavery but continued illegally for an unspecified period of time.

## THE INFRASTRUCTURE OF PLACE

The main concern for the merchants was safely receiving and sending goods and because of this key infrastructure was put in place at the port through 'the ambitious and financially speculative construction of the dock system' (Crowley, 2012, p. 3). A further concern was the transportation of goods either overseas through shipping or in-land by roads, rivers, and canals. The nearest city for business was Manchester 34 miles away. Transport between Liverpool and Manchester was by road and stagecoach, which was in operation from 1757 and was ill-suited for the transportation of quantities of goods. Liverpool also improved the navigability of its existing waterways and built new ones, which included the opening of the first section of the Leeds–Liverpool canal to Wigan in 1774. The following century the Liverpool and Manchester Railway was the first inter-city railway, to open in the world in 1830. The railway provided access to the industrial heartland which infiltrated 'the trade of the greater part of England' (Muir, 2013, p. 232). Liverpool Port also continued to expand its dock and quay areas. Between 1824 and 1858 more than 140 acres of new docks, with 10 miles of quay space, were opened. The major new development was the Albert Dock which opened in 1846, and while it was neither the first nor the biggest of its kind, with its 'innovative port technology' it was the most advanced (Hargan, 2007, p. 44).

What the civil engineer Jesse Hartley and the architect Philip Hardwick created was a new type of modern dock technology, warehousing, and port management system. The Albert Dock was the first enclosed non-combustible dock warehouse system in the world; it also enabled the loading and unloading of ship's cargoes onto the quays which had been built to accommodate ships with cargo capacities of up to 1000 tons. The Albert Dock also was fitted with hydraulic warehouse hoists for lifting goods to the upper floors. The basement vaults were allocated for storing longer-term cargo. The dock and warehouse complex was officially opened by its namesake—Albert, Prince Consort, husband of Queen Victoria. The event marked the first occasion in Liverpool's history in which a member of the Royal Family made a state visit that was marked by major celebrations. What it illustrated was that the new industrial maritime development was about spectacle, this was not about palaces it was about working buildings and is why: 'Warehouses were among the architectural showpieces of the Industrial Revolution' (Stratton & Trinder, 1997,

p. 90). What the Albert Dock contributed to was Liverpool's export market. 'By 1857, the value of Liverpool's export trade mounted to 45% of the UK total, (London's share was 23% and Hull's 13%)' (Dugdale & Fleming, 2012, p. 20).

Productivity went in tandem with imperial expansion. The question is had there been no Industrial Revolution would the Empire have existed in the way that it did, and is why J. R. Ward asks: 'To what extent was its imperial expansion a consequence of its industrial revolution, perhaps through the need for enlarged markets and raw material supplies?' (Ward, 1994, p. 44). If the Industrial Revolution gave rise to the Empire, it also gave rise to Capitalism. Karl Marx's *Capital: A Critique of Political Economy* (1867) aimed 'to examine the capitalist mode of production, and the conditions of production and exchange corresponding to that mode' (Marx, 1909, p. 13). The socioeconomic critique draws on the changing working practices in England that extend to other parts of Britain from the tanners in the northeast of the Scottish Highlands to the pillow lace makers in Devon in the southwest of England. Marx focuses on England and Britain because as James Symonds and Eleanor C. Casella assert: 'Britain was the first industrial nation' (Symonds & Casella, 2006, p. 143). Liverpool was one of its industrial cities and like its other cities things changed in the twentieth century.

## THE TWENTIETH CENTURY

While the Albert Dock was heralded as a feat of modernity, within 50 years of opening it was unable to accommodate the new deeper-hulled steamships. The issue was that the scale of the warehouse development made rebuilding impossible. What had been 'one of the great monuments of c19 engineering; its sublime grandeur unquestionably the climax of Liverpool docks' by the start of the twentieth century had gone into decline (Sharples, 2004, p. 103). The Albert Dock closed in 1972, and many of the warehouses fell largely derelict. 'In spite of this, and somewhat paradoxically, Liverpool became something of an archetype of the de-industrializing city in Britain whilst also pointing to problems in contemporary and historical understandings of economic change' (Andrews, 2020, p. 237). By the early 1980s, the Albert Dock was in a poor state of repairs, as is indicated by Gordon Jackson writing at that time 'to describe its present condition as a national disgrace would be rather charitable' (Jackson, 1983, p. 160). Spurred on by social unrest, Liverpool became part of a Conservative government's Urban Development Corporation flagship scheme to stimulate development in its run-down inner-city areas which had suffered from de-industrialisation and economic decline. The Merseyside Development Corporation (MDC) redeveloped an area of 865 acres and capitalised on the 'waterfront location and the opportunities for stimulating private enterprise activity in commercial, industrial, housing and tourism developments' (Adcock, 1984, p. 288).

One of the issues that the MDC faced was that it was a government initiative. With the level of inner-city decline and social unrest, there was a visible dislike of the government which is why new ways of socially engaging with the public were deployed. The development 'received a major boost with the subsequent opportunity to stage Britain's first international garden festival' (Theokas, 2004, p. 145). The Liverpool International Garden Festival involved reclaiming a derelict industrial site in the southeast of the city, most of which had belonged to the Herculaneum Dock with the remainder having been used as a garbage tip. The Garden Festival was undertaken as a community project which showcased 'different events and exhibitions from different nations in an attempt to make new connections between British cities and the wider world' (Wetherell, 2022, p. 86). Sam Wetherell adds the 'cosmopolitanism repressed an urban social order that was profoundly structured by race in places like Liverpool, a city whose associations with empire and whose history of black, Chinese, and Irish migration were largely overlooked by festival planners' (Wetherell, 2022, p. 86). Despite this being the case, the initiative helped to launch the regeneration of the city.

At the core of the regeneration was the city's maritime history of which the Albert Dock was an integral part. Within the Albert Dock redevelopment was the former Pilotage Building which originally opened in 1883 to help pilot ships entering and leaving the river Mersey, which closed in 1978. The Merseyside Maritime Museum opened in the building in 1980. With the MDC's 'bigger vision,' it was moved to the north warehouse, Block D on the Liverpool Waterfront (Donnellan, 2018, p. 22). The architects Brock Carmichael developed the warehouse site into the Merseyside Maritime Museum, which included the Transatlantic Slavery Gallery in 1994. The expanded International Slavery Museum opened on the third floor in 2007. The new name was due to it 'being an international phenomenon with global consequences' (Benjamin, 2012, p. 178).

The overall industrial appearance of the Merseyside Maritime Museum and the International Slavery Museum was emphasised by the exposed brickwork, cast iron columns, wood beams, arches, stone floors, and planking which are further enhanced by the ambient lighting. The question is: is this an authentic representation of the past or is it something made up? Drawing on the research of Robert D. Sack the question arises: 'Is the site real, or is the real something beneath the surface?' (Sack, 1993, p. 328). A different kind of museum along the quays is Tate Liverpool (formerly the Tate Gallery Liverpool), which opened in a corner warehouse building. 'Keeping alterations to a minimum' was the key requisite of the redesign of the warehouse (Maxwell et al., 1994, p. 133). All these factors attract visitors to Tate Liverpool along with the waterfront location, the Albert Docks's historic environment and the museum's brand name. What was important about the creation of Tate Liverpool and the Merseyside Maritime Museum is that they were 'a catalyst for further investment in the refurbishment of other parts of the dock complex' (Couch & Farr, 2000, 157).

A further consideration concerning the Albert Dock is that it forms the largest collection of warehouse buildings and docking complexes in a single collection of heritage-listed buildings in Britain. After the work of the MDC was completed, Liverpool City Council decided to capitalise on its heritage and applied to UNESCO (United Nations Educational, Scientific and Cultural Organization) for its prestigious World Heritage List. Given the nature of its industrial maritime heritage, at the time of the application, David Keys wrote: 'There have been a few relatively small industrial sites on the World Heritage List for years, including the original icons of industrial archaeology, the eighteenth-century Ironbridge complex in England and the Völklingen Iron Works in Germany' (Keys, 2003, p. 64). In 2004 the city was awarded the World Heritage listing 'Liverpool—Maritime Mercantile City' by UNESCO. The listing was because of the city's historic centre and docklands, and emergence as one of the world's major trading centres in the eighteenth and nineteenth centuries. It was also because of its role as a major port for the mass movement of people, from slaves to emigrants. It also achieved the listing because of its pioneering dock technology, transport systems, and port management (UNESCO, 2004, https://whc.unesco.org/en/list/1150/). By the time of the UNESCO listing most of the heritage sites had been repurposed and contributes to Jessica Moody's assertion that the city is 'a place that *has* had more overt, repeated, and permanent interventions through memorialization, public history, and heritage than anywhere else in Britain' (Moody, 2020, p. 6).

## REINVENTING LIVERPOOL: NEW PLACEMAKING

The attractions at the Albert Dock promote a different history of Liverpool with The Beatles Story Museum, located at the Britannia Vaults which opened 1 May 1990. The marketing states: 'Be transported on an incredible immersive journey as we tell the story of how four young lads from Liverpool were propelled to the dizzy heights of fame and fortune from their humble childhood beginnings' (Beatles Story Museum, 2024, https://www.beatlesstory.com/). The exhibit includes a mock-up of the Cavern Club with a stage where the band first performed in 1961. There is also a reconstruction of Matthew Street, the site of the Cavern Club where fans can walk down memory lane. Despite the celebrity of the Beatles and efforts to focus on its music scene, the Albert Dock is about its maritime heritage. Nearby other areas have also capitalised on this history including the Baltic Triangle, which was a former industrial area around Jamaica Street that markets itself as a 'creative, digital and independent district of Liverpool' (Baltic Triangle, 2024, https://baltictriangle. co.uk/). The Baltic Triangle, the Merchants Quarter, and the Albert Dock are about reimagining the city's heritage through their connection with 'one of the most internationally recognisable waterfronts' in the world (Boland, 2008, p. 358). What all these sites contributed to was the government's vision in recognising that regeneration 'can be a powerful driver for economic growth, attracting investment and tourism, and providing a focus for successful regeneration' (HM Government, 2010, p. 1).

Despite the Albert Dock's redevelopment, by the early 2000s, the city centre had become undesirable. A boost to the city's economy was through the opening of Liverpool One in 2008 which 'is a retail-led, mixed-use development' (Littlefield, 2009, p. 241). The project involved the redevelopment of 42 acres of land in the city centre. What it has become is a privately owned public space (POPS). How it is configured is through Liverpool City Council maintaining a 5% share while the land is on a 250-year lease to a private developer. The scheme completed in 2008 with the aim to create a new kind of 'place branding' for the city (Daramola-Martin, 2009, p. 301). A further boost to the economy was when Liverpool was awarded the joint European Capital of Culture award along with Stavanger in Norway, which resulted in 'substantial European Commission investment' being injected into the city (Parkinson, 2019, pp. 4–5). A different kind of change was underway prior to Liverpool being awarded the European Capital of Culture title. From 2006 UNESCO began raising concerns about Liverpool's proposed modern developments on the riverside, which it feared would detract from the historic setting that had contributed to it being placed on UNESCO's World Heritage List.

Despite UNESCO's various pleas to Liverpool City Council the situation did not abate. 'Only in June 2019, UNESCO requested a moratorium on further large scale development' (Kinsella, 2021, p. 2.). There was no moratorium. The outcome was that Liverpool's UNESCO's World Heritage Listing was deleted in 2021 'due to the irreversible loss of attributes conveying the outstanding universal value of the property' (UNESCO, 2021, https://whc.unesco.org/en/news/2314). The initial development that raised concern was the relocation of Everton Football Club from its 'spiritual home' in Goodison Park to Bramley-Moore Dock, where a state-of-the-art stadium is being built (Georgantas & Lekakis, 2021, p. 277). This decision was unanimously supported by Liverpool City Council. The redevelopment has included demolishing existing buildings and structures on the Bramley-Moore Dock site. The principal development that caused further concern for UNESCO is Liverpool Waters which is being built in an area north of the historic Pier Head on docks that were part of UNESCO's heritage buildings. The residential, business, and leisure development costing £5.5 bn will extend to over 2 km along the banks of the river Mersey and is part of a 30-year plan to transform the city's northern docks.

While Liverpool City Council was criticised for its position to its maritime heritage, UNESCO has also been called out for its lack of flexibility towards new developments. 'Many local authorities see UNESCO as a far-away watchdog that is insufficiently adept in responding to the challenges and demands of modern globalised cities. [...] UNESCO in practice upholds a relatively traditional "preservationist" view on heritage, which increasingly forms an obstacle for urban development projects' (Zwegers, 2022, p. 267). Is UNESCO stuck in the past concerning heritage or is it important that there is watchdog that preserves these sites for future generations? On the question of heritage and Liverpool City Council while money was a driving factor in its decision to turn its back on its maritime heritage, it may also have wanted to distance itself from Liverpool's maritime past. One of the ways to do this was to get rid of it which is what it is presently happening at the former northern docks.

Liverpool City Council initially supported its maritime heritage sites; however, there was a missing factor. 'Liverpool had not sufficiently developed or promoted its World Heritage status and had made less of it than other UK cities such as Edinburgh or Bath' (Parkinson, 2019, p. 160). Why didn't Liverpool promote its World Heritage status in the same way as Edinburgh and Bath? One factor may be that these cities were not involved in the slave trade, although it is likely some of their wealthier families may have had connections with it, but not in the same way as for Liverpool. While the Albert Dock was built decades after the Abolition of the Slave trade, there is the case that money from the eighteenth century was passed down into the nineteenth century that helped to fund it.

The question is: is Liverpool City Council wanting to create new memories through remapping its historic cityscape? The year after the UNESCO Heritage Site listing was removed the Heseltine Institute for Public Policy and Practice re-assessed the historic maritime area. 'Albert Dock is an iconic Liverpool landmark—physically, economically, and politically. For almost two centuries its fortunes have reflected those of the city itself' (Parkinson & Lord, 2017, p. 8). No mention was made as to how Liverpool's history, heritage, and fortune were connected to the slave trade. Is the aim, therefore, to market a more sanitised account of the city? The problem in re-writing history is that it becomes about forgetting. Contested history begins by forgetting. 'Here, forgetting practices include stopping, interfering, preventing, hampering, intruding, opposing, doing nothing, failing to engage, and replacing places of memory as well as mis-remembering the events' (Shin & Jin, 2021, p. 439). While history may forget, the past does not. The question is: how are we remembering these landmarks? When they were constructed, they were part of an 'industrially advanced' society that bankrolled the Empire but failed the nation (Habermas, 1989, p. 1). For this reason, the spaces of Liverpool's past need to be remembered, for future generations 'to promote the heritage of their ancestors and to formulate demands to redress past wrongs' (Araujo, 2012, p. 15).

The Albert Dock was rebranded the Royal Albert Dock in 2018. The paradox is that the Royal Albert Dock appears somehow more able than the Albert Dock to expunge the darker aspects of Liverpool's past. The Royal Albert Dock belongs to a more sanitised account of Liverpool's history and requires agency as this kind of forgetting does not happen by accident. 'Forgetting, after all, is a more complex activity than simply not remembering; it implies a number of procedures' (Vidler, 1992, p. 180).

The procedures that Anthony Vidler identifies require history to be rewritten in a way that removes the more unsavoury moments of its past. If this happens, the ghosts of the past will be muted through 'the silencing of their voices and [...] of their writing out from history' (Frosh, 2013, p. 4). The reality is that these things cannot be resolved this way. The problem that Patrick Wright identities is that the past becomes: 'Restaged and reappropriated' (Wright, 2009, p. 74). The conundrum for the city is that the Royal Albert Dock attracts visitors and businesses because of its heritage and notably its built heritage. Simon Thurley identifies that 'Built heritage is seen as one of the most important assets the nation has in terms of tourism' (Thurley, 2013, p. 257). What built heritage provides is an immersive experience and the offer to interact with the spaces of the past. This can become, however, the architecture of forgetting, and while what has been done cannot be undone what lurks beneath Liverpool's history is its haunted past.

## References

Adcock, B. (1984). Regenerating Merseyside Docklands: The Merseyside Development Corporation 1981–1984. *Town Planning Review*, *55*(3), 265–289. https://doi.org/10.3828/tpr.55.3.r143m60627558776

Andrews, A. (2020). Dereliction, Decay and the Problem of De-industrialization in Britain, c. 1968–1977. *Urban History*, *47*(2), 236–256. https://doi.org/10.1017/S0963926819000245

Araujo, A. L. (2012). Transnational Memory of Slave Merchants: Making the Perpetrators Visible in the Public Space. In A. L. Araujo (Ed.), *Politics of Memory: Making Slavery Visible in the Public Space* (pp. 15–34). Routledge. https://doi.org/10.4324/9780203119075

Baltic Triangle. (2024). (Explore and Discover Liverpool's Creative District). https://baltictriangle.co.uk/

Benjamin, R. (2012). Museums and Sensitive Histories: The International Slavery Museum. In A. L. Araujo (Ed.), *Politics of Memory: Making Slavery Visible in the Public Space* (pp. 178–196). Routledge. https://doi.org/10.4324/9780203119075

Boland, P. (2008). The Construction of Images of People and Place: Labelling Liverpool and Stereotyping Scousers. *Cities*, *25*(6), 355–369. https://doi.org/10.1016/j.cities.2008.09.003

Bonehill, J. (2008). Reynolds' Portrait of Lieutenant-Colonel Banastre Tarleton and the Fashion for War. *Journal for Eighteenth–Century Studies*, *24*(2), 123–144. https://doi.org/10.1111/j.1754-0208.2001.tb00433.x

Brown, A. D., Kramer, M. E., Romano, T. A., & Hirst, W. (2012). Forgetting Trauma: Socially Shared Retrieval-induced Forgetting and Post-traumatic Stress Disorder. *Applied Cognitive Psychology, 26*(1), 24–34. https://doi.org/10.1002/acp.1791

Casey, E. S. (2007). Boundary, Place, and Event in the Spatiality of History. *Rethinking History, 11*(4), 507–512.

Couch, C., & Farr, S. (2000). Museums, Galleries, Tourism and Regeneration: Some Experiences from Liverpool. *Built Environment, 26*(2), 152–163.

Crowley, T. (2012). *Scouse: A Social and Cultural History.* Liverpool University Press. https://doi.org/10.5949/upo9781846317781

Daramola-Martin, A. (2009). Liverpool One and the Transformation of a City: Place Branding, Marketing and the Catalytic Effects of Regeneration and Culture on Repositioning Liverpool. *Place Branding and Public Diplomacy, 5*(4), 301–311. https://doi.org/10.1057/pb.2009.19

Donnellan, C. (2018). *Towards Tate Modern: Public Policy, Private Vision.* Routledge. https://doi.org/10.4324/9781315550503

Dugdale, J., & Fleming, D. (2012). *Liverpool: The Story of a City.* Liverpool University Press.

Earle, P. (2015). *The Earles of Liverpool: A Georgian Merchant Dynasty.* Liverpool University Press. https://doi.org/10.5949/liverpool/9781781381731.001.0001

Egerton, J. (1998). *The British Paintings: National Gallery Catalogues* (distributed by Yale University Press). National Gallery Publications.

Frosh, S. (2013). *Hauntings: Psychoanalysis and Ghostly Transmissions.* Palgrave Macmillan. https://doi.org/10.1057/9781137031259

Georgantas, E., & Lekakis, N. (2021). The Politics of Urban Regeneration in Liverpool and Everton FC's Alternate New Stadium-project Plans. *Regional Studies, Regional Science, 8*(1), 273–290. https://doi.org/10.1080/21681376.2021.1918573

Habermas, J. (1989). *The Structural Transformation of the Public Sphere: An Inquiry into a Category of Bourgeois Society* (T. Burger, Trans.). Polity Press.

Hargan, J. (2007). Liverpool's Albert Dock: Life on the Merseyside Quays. *British Heritage, 27*(6), 42–49.

HM Government. (2010). *The Government's Statement on the Historic Environment for England.* Department for Culture, Media and Sport.

Jackson, G. (1983). *The History and Archaeology of Ports.* World's Work Ltd.

Jung, C. G. (2001). *On the Nature of the Psyche* (R. F. C. Hull, Trans.). Routledge.

Kelly, M., Ó Gráda, C., & Solar, P. M. (2021). Safety at Sea during the Industrial Revolution. *The Journal of Economic History, 81*(1), 239–275. https://doi.org/10.1017/S0022050720000595

Keys, D. (2003). Assault on Tradition: A UNESCO Nomination Compels a Second Look at the Surprising History of Gritty, Industrial Liverpool. *Archaeology, 56*(6), 64–67.

Kinsella, C. (2021). *Urban Regeneration and Neoliberalism: The Liverpool Home.* Routledge.

Kostyal, K. (2013). Put To The Sword: Banastre Tarleton And His Ruthless British Legion. *Military History, 29*(6), 38–45.

Levecq, C. (2008). *Slavery and Sentiment: The Politics of Feeling in Black Atlantic Antislavery Writing, 1770–1850.* University Press of New England.

Littlefield, D. (2009). *Liverpool One: Remaking of a City Centre.* Wiley.

Marx, M. (1909). *Capital: A Critique of Political Economy,* Volume 1: The Process of Capitalist Production, ed. M. Engels (trans. S. Moore & E. Aveling from 3rd German Ed.), Chicago: Charles H. Kerr & Company.

Maxwell, R., Wilford, M., & Muirhead, T. (1994). *James Stirling Michael Wilford And Associates: Building Projects 1975–1992.* Verlag Gerd Hatje.

McDade, K. (2012). Bristol and Liverpool Port Improvements in the Latter Half of the Eighteenth Century: The Case for Liverpool's Entrepreneurial Success. *International Journal of Maritime History, 24*(2), 201–224. https://doi.org/10.1177/084387141202400209

Moody, J. (2020). *The Persistence of Memory: Remembering Slavery in Liverpool, 'slaving capital of the world'.* Liverpool University Press. https://doi.org/10.2307/j.ctv1675bp5

Morgan, K. (2007a). Liverpool's Dominance in the British Slave Trade, 1740–1807. In D. Richardson, S. Schwarz, & A. Tibbles (Eds.), *Liverpool and Transatlantic Slavery* (pp. 14–42). Liverpool University Press.

Morgan, K. (2007b). *Slavery and the British Empire: From Africa to America.* Oxford University Press.

Muir, R. (2013). *A History of Liverpool* (2nd ed.). Williams & Northgate.

National Museums Liverpool. (2024). (Liverpool and the Transatlantic Slave Trade Information Sheet 3). https://www.liverpoolmuseums.org.uk/archivesheet3

Parkinson, M. (2019). *Liverpool: Beyond the Brink.* Liverpool University Press.

Parkinson, M., & Lord, A. (2017). *Albert Dock: What Part in Liverpool's Continuing Renaissance?* Heseltine Institute for Public Policy and Practice; University of Liverpool.

Royal Museums Greenwich. (2023). (F0886 Plan and Sections of Slave Ship 'Brooks' [Sometimes 'Brookes']), https://images.rmg.co.uk/asset/21421/

Sack, R. D. (1993). The Power of Place and Space. *Geographical Review, 83*(3), 326–329. https://doi.org/10.2307/215735

Sharples, J. (2004). *Liverpool.* Yale University Press.

Shaw, C. (2020). Liverpool's Slave Trade Legacy. *History Today, 70*(3), 15–18.

Shin, H., & Jin, Y. (2021). The Politics of Forgetting: Unmaking Memories and Reacting to Memory-place-making. *Geographical Research, 59*(3), 439–451. https://doi.org/10.1111/1745-5871.12467

Stephenson, R. A. (1955). The Development of the Liverpool Dock System. *Transactions,* (8), 1953–1955, 61–76 printed in Liverpool Nautical Research Society (2019) The Liverpool Dock System, Liverpool: Liverpool Nautical Research Society.

Stratton, M., & Trinder, B. (1997). *Industrial England.* B. T. Batsford.

Symonds, J., & Casella, E. C. (2006). Historical Archaeology and Industrialisation. In D. Hicks & M. C. Beaudry (Eds.), *The Cambridge Companion to Historical Archaeology* (pp. 143–167). Cambridge University Press. https://doi.org/10.1017/CCO9781139167321.009

Taylor, D., & Davenport, T. (2009). *Liverpool: Regeneration of a City Centre.* BDP.

The Beatles Story Museum, Liverpool. (2024). (Welcome To The Beatles Story Museum, Liverpool). https://www.beatlesstory.com/

Theokas, A. C. (2004). *Grounds for Review: The Garden Festival in Urban Planning and Design.* Liverpool University Press.

Thurley, S. (2013). *Men from the Ministry: How Britain Saved Its Heritage.* Yale University Press.

UNESCO. (2004). (Liverpool Maritime City). https://whc.unesco.org/en/list/1150/

UNESCO. (2021). (News: World Heritage Committee deletes Liverpool—Maritime Mercantile City from UNESCO's World Heritage List). https://whc.unesco.org/en/news/2314

Vidler, A. (1992). *The Architectural Uncanny: Essays in the Modern Unhomely.* The MIT Press.

Ward, J. R. (1994). The Industrial Revolution and British Imperialism, 1750–1850. *Economic History Review, 47*(1), 44–65.

Wetherell, S. (2022). Sowing Seeds: Garden Festivals and the Remaking of British Cities after Deindustrialization. *Journal of British Studies, 61*(1), 83–104. https://doi.org/10.1017/jbr.2021.67

Wright, P. (2009). *On Living in an Old Country: The National Past in Contemporary Britain.* Oxford University Press.

Zwegers, D. (2022). *Cultural Heritage in Transition. A Multi-level Perspective on World Heritage in Germany and the United Kingdom, 1970–2020.* Springer.

# Index

**A**

Acquisition/acquisitions,
48–51, 53, 54
Acropolis, 48–50
Africa, 38, 39, 66
African, 67
Albert Dock (Royal Albert Dock),
69–73, 75, 76
Antiquities, 8, 48, 49, 52–54,
56, 58, 59
Appropriation, 5, 8
Arab, 55
Archaeology, 5, 54, 56–59, 72
Architecture, 2, 5, 20, 21, 42,
50–52, 76
Army, 22, 40
Artefact/artefacts,
6, 41, 58
Artists, 3, 33, 51
Assyria, 48, 55
Assyrian, 53, 54
Assyromania, 48
Athens, 49–52, 58, 59
Attica, 51

**B**

Baghdad, 53, 57
Banqueting House, 32–35
Bell, Gertrude, 55–57
Benin Bronzes, 5, 6
Bill of Rights (1689), 8, 36
Black Lives Matter (BLM), 8, 40–42
Bogdanos, Matthew, 57, 58
Borders, 6, 56
Botta, Paul-Émile, 53, 54
*Brideshead Revisited* (1945), 22, 23
Britain, 4–8, 17, 19, 22, 24, 37–42,
48–59, 66, 68, 70–73
British
   British Empire, 22, 38, 56, 68
   British Institute for the Study of
      Iraq (BISI), 57
   British Museum, 6, 8, 48,
      50–54, 57–59
   British Raj, 24
   British School of Archaeology in
      Iraq (BSAI), 57
Building/buildings, 4, 8, 21, 24, 32,
   34, 36–39, 50–52, 67, 69, 72, 74

**C**

Cenotaph, 39–41
Christie, Agatha, 5, 56, 57
Chronicle, 17
Churchill, Winston, 18, 19, 41, 56
City, 8, 15, 20, 24, 40, 42, 48–51, 53, 58, 66, 67, 69–76
Clive, Robert ( Clive of India), 37, 38
Colonial, 5, 23, 37–40, 49, 53, 57, 58, 68
Colonialism, 5, 56, 68
Colonies, 54
Colston, Edward, 41
Contested Histories Initiative (CHI), 2
Contested history, 2–9, 14–22, 24, 25, 32–42, 48–49, 51–53, 57–59, 66–69, 71, 73, 75, 76
Cook, Captain James, 38, 39
Cotton, 66
Country house, 7, 15, 22–25
Court, 7, 32–34, 58
Critical heritage, 2, 4–8, 20, 21, 48, 51, 57–59, 72–76
   *See also* Heritage
Cromwell, Oliver, 35, 36
Culture, 8, 18, 49, 52, 54


**D**

De Certeau, Michel, 19, 25
Destruction, 20, 50, 57
Displacement, 5, 8
Divine Right of Kings, 33–37
Dock/docks, 66, 69, 70, 72, 74


**E**

East India Company, 38
Edwardian, 20
Elgin Marbles, *see* Parthenon Marbles

Empire, 2, 8, 22, 23, 37–40, 52, 67, 70, 71, 75
England, 17, 18, 20, 24, 35, 37, 51, 52, 54, 67, 69, 70, 72
English Civil Wars, 18, 34
Englishness, 22
Enslaved, 67, 68
*Epic of Gilgamesh*, 54
European, 6, 38, 55
Euston, 21
Excavations, 48, 53, 54, 56, 57
Expedition/expeditions, 38, 56
Exploration, 6


**F**

Façade, 21
Fiction, 23
Foreign, 23, 24, 32, 54
Foreign and Commonwealth Office, 39
Foreign, Commonwealth and Development Office, 40
Foucault, Michel, 20
France, 20, 50, 52
French, 37, 39, 49, 53–55
Future, 15, 23, 74, 75


**G**

Geography, 3–4, 6
Gilgamesh, *see Epic of Gilgamesh*
Global, 7, 71
Glorious Revolution, 18, 36
*The Go-Between* (1953), 23, 24
Government, 8, 19–21, 23, 24, 32, 37, 40, 42, 54, 68, 71, 73
Grand narrative/narratives, 2, 4, 6, 18, 19, 22, 25, 49, 51, 58
Greece, 8, 48–59

**H**
Heritage, 4–6, 48–49, 74
  *See also* Critical heritage
Herodotus, 7, 15, 16, 25
Historic environment, 2, 7, 14,
  32, 40, 72
Historicising/historicizing, 7, 14–25
Historiography, 2, 15–16, 25
History, *see* Contested history/
  contested histories

**I**
Imagination, 15, 23, 39, 48
Imperial, 2, 23, 32, 34, 38–40,
  52, 54, 70
Imperialism, 6, 18, 24, 38–42
India, 23, 24, 38, 54
Indian, 24, 37, 38, 55
Industrial Revolution, 8, 20, 69, 70
International, 6, 48, 52, 71
International Slavery Museum, 71, 72
Iraq, 56–58
Iraq Museum, 56, 58
Iron, 66, 72

**J**
James I (of England) James VI of
  Scotland, 33, 34
*The Jewel in the Crown* (1984), 23, 24

**K**
Kensington Palace, 36
Kingdom of Iraq, 56

**L**
Layard, Austen Henry, 48, 53, 54, 57
Liverpool, 8, 9, 21, 66–76

London, 6–8, 20, 21, 32, 35, 39, 41,
  52, 53, 68, 70
Looted, 57, 58
Lord Elgin, 48

**M**
Mallowan, Sir Max Edgar
  Lucien, 56, 57
Maritime, 8, 66, 69, 71–75
Marx, Karl, 70
Memorial/memorials, 38, 39, 41, 49
Memory/memories, 2, 6, 19, 24, 33,
  38, 42, 51, 66, 73, 75
Mercantile, 68
Merseyside Maritime Museum,
  71, 72
Mesopotamia, 8, 48–59
Middle Eastern, 55
Monarchy, 8, 34, 35
Mosul, 53
*Murder in Mesopotamia* (Agatha
  Christie novel), 56
Myth, 2, 15, 16, 51

**N**
Narrative/narratives, *see* Grand
  narrative/narratives
Nation, 5, 6, 8, 18, 23, 38,
  39, 42, 48, 49, 52, 55,
  57, 75, 76
Nimrud, 53, 54
Nineveh, 53, 54, 58
Nostalgia, 22

**O**
Orient, 54
Ottoman, 49, 50, 53
Overseas, 5–8, 40, 69

**P**
Parliament, 8, 33–36, 40
Parthenon, 8, 48–53, 58, 59
Parthenon Marbles, 51, 59
Past, 2, 4–7
Pericles, 49
Place, 2–9, 15, 17, 22, 24, 25, 32–42,
    48–59, 66–76
Plato, 4
Postcolonial, 6
Present, 2, 14, 15, 19, 24, 41, 42, 52,
    57–59, 70
Private, 8, 24, 34, 35, 40, 48, 67, 71, 73
Privately owned public space (POPS), 73
Public, 2, 7, 8, 19, 21, 24, 32, 34, 35,
    38–40, 48, 49, 51–54, 57,
    67, 71, 73


**R**
Racism, 40, 41
Reconstructing, 55–57
Regeneration, 21, 71, 73
Reinventing, 73–76
Remembrance, 39–40
Repatriation, 57
*Rosetta Stone*, 49, 50
Royal Albert Dock, 75, 76
Royal Navy, 36


**S**
St. Pancras, 21
Sculpture/sculptures, 8, 36,
    48–54, 58, 59
Society, 19, 40, 42, 68, 75
Sovereignty, 38, 41
Space, 2–9, 14–25, 32–42, 52, 53,
    55, 66–76
Spatial turn, the, 3, 4
State (the), 2–4, 8, 15, 17–20, 32,
    34–36, 40, 42, 49, 50, 69

Statue/statues, 2, 35–41, 58
Story, 2, 7, 16, 18, 24, 42, 48,
    55, 56, 73
Stuart, 7, 32–34, 36, 37
Sugar, 66


**T**
Territory, 38
Thatcher, Margaret, 19, 21
Thucydides, 7, 15
Trade, 5, 6, 8, 39, 41, 66–70, 75
Tradition, 6, 16–18, 22
Trafalgar Square, 36, 40
Transatlantic, 8, 68
Truth, 14, 16–18
Tuan, Yi-Fu, 3, 4


**U**
United Kingdom (of Great Britain and
    Northern Ireland), 8, 37, 40,
    42, 70, 75
United Nations Educational, Scientific
    and Cultural Organization
    (UNESCO), 72, 74, 75
United States (US), 39, 57, 58
Urban, 2, 3, 20, 40–42, 67, 71, 74


**V**
Victorian, 20, 21
The Victorian Society, 20, 21
Visitor, 8, 55, 72, 76
Voyages, 38, 66, 68


**W**
Westminster, 33, 36
Whitehall, 8, 32–42
Whitehall Palace, 7, 32, 33,
    35, 36, 42

# GPSR Compliance

*The European Union's (EU) General Product Safety Regulation (GPSR) is a set of rules that requires consumer products to be safe and our obligations to ensure this.*

*If you have any concerns about our products, you can contact us on ProductSafety@springernature.com*

In case Publisher is established outside the EU, the EU authorized representative is:

Springer Nature Customer Service Center GmbH
Europaplatz 3
69115 Heidelberg, Germany

The manufacturer's authorised representative in the EU is Springer
Nature Customer Service Centre GmbH, Europaplatz 3, 69115 Heidelberg,
Germany. If you have any concerns regarding our products, please
contact ProductSafety@springernature.com

Printed and bound by CPI Group (UK) Ltd, Croydon, CR0 4YY
29/04/2026
02099531-0003